Adopted By God

Healing Through Connection to the Father

Matt Lambert

His Publishing Services Ltd

Adopted by God: Healing Through Connection to the Father

Copyright © 2025 by Matthieu Lambert.

The right of Matthieu Lambert to be identified as the author of this work has been asserted by him in accordance with the Copyright, Design and Patents Act 1988.

All rights reserved. No part of this book may be reproduced, stored in a retrieval system, or transmitted in any form or by any means—electronic, mechanical, photocopying, recording, or any other—except for brief quotations in printed reviews, without the prior permission of the publisher.

ISBN 978-1-0683748-0-7

All Scripture quotations, unless otherwise indicated, are taken from The Holy Bible, New International Version®, NIV®. Copyright © 1973, 1978, 1984, 2011 by Biblica, Inc.® Used by permission. All rights reserved worldwide.

Scripture quotations marked NLT are taken from the Holy Bible, New Living Translation, copyright © 1996, 2004, 2007, 2015 by Tyndale House Foundation. Used by permission of Tyndale House Publishers, Inc., Carol Stream, Illinois 60188. All rights reserved.

Scripture quotations marked ESV are from The ESV® Bible (The Holy Bible, English Standard Version®), copyright © 2001 by Crossway, a publishing ministry of Good News Publishers. Used by permission. All rights reserved.

Scripture quotations marked NKJV are taken from the New King James Version®. Copyright © 1982 by Thomas Nelson. Used by permission. All rights reserved.

Any internet addresses (websites, etc.) in this book are offered as a resource. They are not intended in any way to be or imply an endorsement by the publisher, nor does the publisher vouch for the content of these sites for the life of this book.

Circle of Security Image in Chapters 1 & 5, used by permission of Circle of Security International. https://www.circleofsecurityinternational.com/

Cover design: Chris Green

Contents

Praise for Adopted by God	1
Acknowledgements	3
Preface	5
Introduction	7

Part I: Bonds that shape us - The journey of connection

1. Forging our early bonds: Reciprocal connection — 11
2. Missing the building blocks of belonging: Insecure childhood foundations — 26
3. How the past influences the present: The mirror of adulthood — 41
4. Breaking the chains: Transforming generational patterns of connection — 55

Part II: Unveiling the Father's heart in relationships

5. Knowing connection to a loving heavenly father — 72
6. Seeing yourself as the Father sees you — 86
7. Examples and warnings from the word — 98

Part III: Healing through connection to the Father

    8. The healing journey begins with spiritual adoption   114

    9. God's healing touch for the child who hurts   128

    10. Reclaiming inner healing and wholeness through cultivating divine intimacy   142

    11. Jesus' perfect connection to God the Father   156

Conclusion   166

Adopted by God is a compelling exploration of the life-changing journey that comes from understanding our adoption into God's family. Matt's deep empathy and clarity of the subject matter as he shares his personal experiences are so helpful in revealing how our relationship with God shapes and heals our identities.

This book integrates the complexities of how we make and maintain emotional bonds with a rich depth of biblical teaching. It shows how understanding our adoption by God can bring about profound emotional healing, peace and a stronger sense of identity. Throughout my years in ministry, helping people discover their identity in God, I have often observed that certain methods, even if not always fully understood, produce significant results. This book offers a fresh perspective on why these methods work by revealing how our early relationships affect our daily interactions with our children, spouse, family and everyone we connect with and most importantly, our relationship with God.

Adopted by God is a fantastic book that helpfully bridges the gap between theology and psychology, making it a valuable resource for any Christian.

Andy Robinson, Pastor, Educator, Influencer, Founder of WayMaker.org.uk

Adopted by God is a profoundly insightful and hope-filled read. Matt Lambert weaves personal insights, biblical wisdom and practical tools into a compelling narrative. This book is a gift to adoptive and foster families and indeed all readers searching for deeper relational and spiritual connection. Matt emphasises that understanding our adoption into God's family leads to a restored identity, wholeness and an intimate relationship with the Father. It will inspire and equip readers to embrace their identity as beloved children of God.

Tarn Bright, Co-CEO of Safe Families & Home for Good

Adopted by God is a beautifully crafted book. It weaves into the story of attachment: wisdom from bible characters; lessons from Matt's journey; prayers and questions. This helps the reader to explore their own life and move closer towards restoration and a greater closeness with our Father God. I would highly recommend to adopters, foster carers and those who want to take the deeper challenges of life and use it for the good of others.

Mary Penberthy, co-leader of a Christian adoption & fostering support group, former foster carer & adopter

Adopted by God is a profound work that deeply resonated with me. As I explored Matt's analogies, I found myself reflecting on my own upbringing and how I can relate to the issue of trust. It made me think about the significant impact that trust, or the lack of it, can have on a person's life—something I know only too well. I am deeply thankful to Jesus for breaking that cycle in my life, allowing me to move beyond the hurt and raise my children with an awareness of the damage I experienced. They are learning from my journey, which brings a sense of healing and hope.

Rachael Shalloe-Cooper, Pioneer Location Leader for Create Church

ACKNOWLEDGEMENTS

This book would not have been possible without the support and encouragement of many people.

First, my heartfelt thanks to **Steve Bavington**, a close friend who helped bring the idea of *Adopted by God* to life. It was during a conversation at a local café, where Steve wrote the title on a napkin, that this journey began. Thank you for holding me accountable and pushing me to follow through on that initial spark.

I'm deeply grateful to **Simon Holley**, my coach, who has walked with me through the writing process. From shaping my ideas to guiding me through each step, your insights and wisdom have been instrumental in bringing this book to completion.

I also want to thank **Denise Bellingham-Young**, a dear friend from Grace Church, I can't thank you enough for the time, effort and heart you've poured into this project. Your support has gone far beyond the pages, offering personal encouragement and guidance at every turn. The countless hours you've spent editing, discussing ideas, and helping me make this a truly special project mean more to me than I can express. This book carries your imprint in so many ways, and I am profoundly grateful for your dedication and friendship.

A special thank you to **Laura Mayor and Beanie (Lee Anne Ketcham)** from Grace Church Wolverhampton for their thoughtful insights and help with copyediting. Your time and attention have been invaluable, not only in refining the manuscript, but also in making sure the language and message of the book stayed true to its purpose. I deeply appreciate the care and effort you both put into this.

A big thank you to **my parents** who have shaped me into the man that I am today, for better and for worse, through those early connections and their love and care.

To my children, **Jamie and Gracie**, I owe deep thanks. Without you I would know nothing of the lessons learned in this book. You are the reason I've had to grow and learn so much and my life is immeasurably richer because of it. This book exists because of the journey we've been on together.

And most importantly, to my wife, **Rachel Lambert,** there are not enough words to express my gratitude. Your love, support and incredible attention to detail have been vital to this book's quality, but even more than that, your belief in me has sustained me through this entire journey. You've patiently stood by me, cheering me on at every stage, and your strength and wisdom inspire me daily. This book is as much yours as it is mine, and I am constantly in awe of the woman God has made you to be. Thank you for being my greatest encourager, my anchor and my partner in everything. I love you deeply, and I am forever grateful for your presence in my life.

To everyone who has walked alongside me on this journey, thank you for your prayers, encouragement and belief in the vision behind this book. I am deeply grateful.

Preface

When my wife and I began the adoption process over a decade ago, I never imagined it would lead me to write a book. While preparing for the adoption of our son, we attended training focused on the psychological and emotional needs of children. I was struck by how many of the concepts aligned with theological truths. I began to see parallels between adoption and the way God adopts us into His family. As the training continued, I realised that these insights weren't relevant just to parenting, but also deeply tied to our relationship with God.

As an adoptive father of two children, I've experienced the joys and complexities of adoption first-hand. Though the details of my children's stories are theirs to tell (and therefore not detailed in this book), our journey has profoundly shaped my understanding of relationships—both human and divine. But what I quickly discovered is that you don't have to be adopted or an adoptive parent to face struggles with connection. The same challenges adoptive parents encounter in building trust and connection with their children, are challenges many of us experience in our own relationships and even in our spiritual lives.

This idea became even more real to me after our second adoption, which brought unique challenges for our family. Through therapy sessions and the process of writing this book, I began to learn surprising things about myself. I had always believed my primary love language was acts of service, but discovered it was actually physical touch. This was just one of many realisations that emerged as I confronted my own attachment history. I began to see how unresolved wounds from my past were shaping not just my role as a father, but also my connection to God and the people around me.

This book is the product of years of reflection, research and personal growth. My goal is not just to explore the connections we form through adoption, but to look at how early relational experiences—whether through family, friendships, or life's challenges—shape our ability to connect with others and with God. In Scripture, I found patterns that reflect these same struggles, showing that this is a journey we all share in one way or another.

In writing *Adopted by God*, I've made a point to avoid complicated jargon, keeping the material accessible for anyone. The ideas are deep, but I present them in a way that is meant to be approachable and personal. My aim is to share insights I've gained—not just about adoption, but about what it means to be adopted into the family of God, and how that truth can bring healing and transformation, no matter your story.

This journey has brought me to a place of seeking deeper connection, both with God and with others. I invite you to join me in exploring how early relationships shape our sense of identity and belonging. My hope is that you will find healing and encouragement as we learn together what it means to live out the fullness of being adopted by God.

Introduction

Do you sometimes feel alone, like you don't quite belong? Or do you struggle with emotional insecurity that just won't go away? You're not the only one. Many of us carry wounds from our past—wounds that shape how we see ourselves and how we relate to others, including our relationship with God. These wounds can come from anywhere: difficult family relationships, life's unexpected hardships, or moments of feeling rejected or unseen. Whatever your story, the journey to healing rests in understanding the power of spiritual adoption and finding our secure place in the embrace of our heavenly Father. Healing comes through a deep connection to God, who meets us exactly where we are.

I've walked this path myself, wrestling with feelings of not belonging and struggling to connect with others. For years, I felt misunderstood and isolated, not feeling like I belonged and having no sense of self. This impacted my self-esteem, how I related to the world and my relationships with those around me. I share my story with you to show that healing is possible. I've seen transformation in my life; you can experience transformation too.

As an adoptive parent, I've also seen firsthand how early bonds—or the lack thereof—profoundly affect our lives. Our children didn't get the best start and that has shaped their journey toward healing. When you have a child through natural birth, you leave the hospital and figure things out as you go. But as adoptive parents, my wife and I received extensive training and support because adopted children need specific approaches to help them heal and connect. What surprised me was how much of that training applied to all relationships—not just with our children, but with each other, with ourselves and with God.

We've read countless books on adoption and parenting children with special needs. We're currently in therapy, learning how our own relational histories impact the way we connect with our kids. But along the way, I've realised that the same patterns—of trust, attachment and healing—are at work in our spiritual lives. You don't have to be an adoptive parent to feel the effects of broken trust or distant relationships. Many of us carry wounds that shape how we approach God, even if we don't realise it. The Apostle Paul uses the term "spiritual adoption" to describe how we come into God's family. Just as adoptive parents work to build trust and connection with their children, God invites us into a deep, healing relationship with Him.

I believe that sharing insights from psychology and Scripture can help guide you towards emotional and spiritual healing. Our early relationships shape our ability to trust and connect, influencing every aspect of our lives. By exploring these dynamics, we can understand how to overcome past wounds and build a stronger, more intimate relationship with God.

Together, we will delve into how our early attachments affect our present, how God nurtures us as his adopted children, and how embracing this divine relationship can transform our lives. Through real-life stories—both personal and biblical—you will see the practical outworking of these ideas, finding hope and encouragement for your own journey.

By reading on, you'll learn to understand yourself better. You will discover how to reclaim inner healing and wholeness by connecting more deeply with God. You'll find tools to heal from your past and experience God's love in a whole new way. This journey can change your life, helping you feel secure, valued and deeply loved.

This is an invitation to discover the healing power of spiritual adoption. An invitation to reclaim your identity, finding security in God's love, and experiencing the profound sense of belonging that comes from being his child. As you embark on this journey, you will learn to embrace God's unconditional love, heal from your past, and walk confidently into the future he has for you.

Healing your past is crucial for your personal and spiritual growth. Through a deep connection with God, you can experience the transformative relationship that comes from being adopted by him. Begin this journey right now towards a deeper intimacy with God. Understand how healing can lead to a life filled with God's love and a secure sense of belonging.

Part I: Bonds that shape us - The journey of connection

His Publishing Services Ltd

Chapter 1

Forging our early bonds: Reciprocal connection

Don't ask me why, but I don't remember a lot from my childhood. What I do remember are the times spent in the kitchen with my mum—stirring a pot of spaghetti bolognese, rolling out pastry for mince pies at Christmas. We brewed ginger beer in the summer and elderberry wine in the autumn, and we'd often make jams and marmalades, the kitchen filled with the smells of bubbling sugar and spices.

I remember games of chess with my dad, playing bridge with the whole family and time spent learning about computers at a time when they were just becoming something people had at home. But those moments weren't just about the food, the games or the excitement of the tech. They were about being together—the laughter, the quiet concentration and the simple feeling of being safe.

Looking back, I realise my passion for cooking, baking and brewing isn't just about the creative process. Though that is a big part of it, it's also about something deeper: how these activities help me feel connected—not just to the people I share them with, but to something bigger. I believe we're created in the image of a Creator God, and when I'm in the kitchen, I feel like I'm reflecting a small part of that creativity.

Those early experiences taught me what it feels like to be close to someone, to be seen and to belong. Similarly, my love for games has carried over into my adult life. I still enjoy games nights with my friends Chris and Hannah and their children, all avid gamers. It's not just about games—it's about connection. And it has often led to late night dog walks where Chris and I have chewed the fat and reflected on how complicated our lives can be.

It's in these ordinary moments—over meals, shared laughter and the simple act of being together—that healthy connections are often built. For some, these early bonds with caregivers create a deep sense of security, shaping how we see ourselves and the world around us. When those connections are strong, we grow up knowing we're loved, valued and safe. These early relationships play a crucial role in how we relate to others, not just in the past but also shaping our present and influencing our future,

> It is important that we know where we come from, because if you do not know where you come from, then you don't know where you are, and if you don't know where you are, you don't know where you're going. And if you don't know where you're going, you're probably going wrong.

In this quote from *I Shall Wear Midnight*, Terry Pratchett poignantly frames life as a journey with a beginning, a present and a destination. If our present circumstances feel off, it might be because we started from the wrong place or need a better understanding of our origins to reach our desired destination. Something about where or how we began fundamentally impacts everything that follows in life's journey. Much of this has to do with the first relationships we formed right at the start.

Early bonds with a caregiver

A caregiver and their child develop a deep, emotional, mutually satisfying bond in infancy. They form a reciprocal connection of positive interactions to help the infant to start to give sense to what they hear, see, touch, taste and smell. At this stage, the infant is incapable of experiencing things for themselves. They experience the world through the eyes of their primary caregiver. They smile when the caregiver smiles and laugh when they laugh. They learn to copy the facial expressions of the person sitting opposite them and take their cues from them. These early exchanges shape the child's perceptions of and interactions with the world. This defines the term "attachment".

The Cambridge Dictionary defines attachment as "a feeling of love and need for another person, for example, for a mother by her child." But attachment is about more than just love; it's about a connection that flows back and forth between two people, almost like a dance. Dan Hughes, a well-known clinical psychologist, has considerable expertise in this area. He begins the preface of his book *Building the Bonds of Attachment* with a description of what a mutually satisfying bond should look like:

In healthy families, a baby forms a secure attachment with her parents as naturally as she breathes, eats, smiles and cries. This occurs easily because of her parents' attuned interactions with her. Her parents notice her physiological affective states and they respond to her sensitively and fully. Beyond simply meeting her unique needs, however, her parents 'dance' with her. Hundreds of times, day after day, they dance with her.[1]

---

1. Dan Hughes, *Building the Bonds of Attachment,* 2nd. Ed. (Lanham MD: Jason Aronson, 2006) p. ix

As a Christian, when I hear this, my mind is immediately drawn to Zephaniah 3:17: "The Lord your God is with you, the Mighty Warrior who saves. He will take great delight in you; in his love, he will no longer rebuke you, but will rejoice over you with singing." The Bible tells us that the Lord rejoices over us with singing and takes great delight in doing so. This, too, speaks of a reciprocal connection between us and God. In the children's book *The Garden, the Curtain and the Cross*, the author considers what it would have been like to be present in the Garden of Eden before sin entered the world: "In the garden, everything was wonderful. The world was full of laughing and playing and smiling and fun. There was nothing bad, ever. There was no one sad ever. And best of all... God was there...People could see God, speak to God and just enjoy being with God. It was wonderful to live with God."[2] This was the original design for the relationship between God and humanity.

Similarly, looking forward to the new heavens and new earth in Revelation 21:3, the apostle John says, "And I heard a loud voice from the throne saying, 'Look! God's dwelling place is now among the people, and he will dwell with them. They will be his people, and God himself will be with them and be their God.'" The Bible starts and finishes with a depiction of a reciprocal connection with God. Everything else in between is his story (or history) of restoring the bond lost at the fall in Genesis 3. We are, however, getting ahead of ourselves a little. We will return in depth to explore the nature of divine connection when we consider what the Bible says about God's role in our lives as primary caregiver. We start by examining the impact of our early bonds with a natural caregiver from an earthly perspective, then move to a biblical and supernatural view.

---

2. Carl Laferton, *The Garden, The Curtain and the Cross* (The Good Book Company, 2016)

The cycle of connection

Attachment is about the early bonds forged between a caregiver and a child, within which, a mutual exchange of giving and taking develops. This dynamic and responsive interaction between the caregiver and the child builds emotional connection and security. For that to happen, both parties must be engaged and present in the moment, responding to each other's cues and needs.

Early in the relationship, the only way an infant can express its needs is by crying. The back and forth between them goes something like this:

- The child experiences a need–this could be hunger, discomfort from a soiled nappy, fear, or a need for reassurance and closeness.

- The child cries to express that need.

- The caregiver establishes the facts to respond to the child's needs. Precisely determining what need the child is expressing may require some trial and error. Once they know why the child is crying, they respond accordingly to meet the need.

- The child feels OK. When the caregiver meets the need, trust develops.

- The child stops crying, and the cycle is complete.

This attachment cycle of expressing and responding to needs repeats throughout the day.

As the caregiver consistently responds to the child's needs, the child learns to trust. They realise the caregiver will respond quickly and appropriately when they cry. A bond of trust develops through this consistent caregiving. This cycle affects what the child believes and expects of themselves and others. Through this exchange they learn to trust or mistrust. This bond is a significant factor, if not the main factor, in shaping their relational future and how they will interact with others as they grow up. If the primary relationship they forged with their caregiver is a relationship of trust, then they will likely be more naturally inclined to trust others. Trust must be established early on to ensure they trust in subsequent relationships and they will be less worried about how people will respond to them.

Pathways in the brain

This illustrates how the brain forms pathways upon which information travels. To help us understand this notion, picture the brain as a big city with many roads and streets. The roads are like pathways helping the information travel from one part of the brain to another. Your brain builds new roads whenever you learn to do something new or improve your skills through practice.

Learning to ride a bike is a great example. When you first learn to ride a bike, your brain builds a pathway to help you remember how to ride. This becomes hard-wired into your brain. So even if you haven't ridden one for years, when you pick a bike up again, you instinctively know what to do because your brain formed a specific pathway. This explains why we commonly use the expression, 'It's like riding a bike.' Learning to trust is like riding a bike.

New experiences shape our minds. Each one forges fresh pathways, rewiring our brains in remarkable ways. Someone who formed healthy early bonds displays confidence in going out and exploring the world. They are constantly trying new things, thereby creating new pathways in their brain. As a result, their brain structure changes, with more connections and efficiency. This promotes mental growth and the acquisition of new skills. And the more you practise those skills, the easier it gets. Practice leads to those pathways in the brain being smoother and faster. Continuing with the example of riding a bike, the initial journey travels along a gravel path with many bumps and potholes. As you grow in your confidence and ability to ride well, the pathway in your brain becomes smoother and faster. Eventually, the pathway resembles a smooth, fast highway upon which the information travels efficiently and quickly.

The more you practise something, the more the pathways in your brain are strengthened, making it easier to remember and perform the skill. This applies to trust. As the child's needs are met consistently, they learn to trust their caregiver. A pathway of trust forms in their brain. Over time, the ongoing relationship of trust with their caregiver reinforces and strengthens this pathway. They develop an inclination to trust others as they form a vital pathway of trust in those early bonds.

Mutual connection

Dr John Bowlby, a British psychiatrist, initially developed attachment theory. He was the first professional to articulate how important the early bonds we forge are to our relational experience throughout the whole of life:

> Intimate attachments to other human beings are the hub around which a person's life revolves, not only as an infant or a toddler or a schoolchild but throughout adolescence and years of maturity as well, and on into old age. From these intimate attachments, a person draws strength and enjoyment of life and, through what he contributes, gives strength and enjoyment to others.[3]

---

3. John Bowlby, *Attachment and Loss: Volume 1. Attachment* (New York: Basic Books, 1980), p.40.

Again, this hints at deeper psychological and emotional meaning to these connections beyond just the physical needs. A mutual, shared understanding between the primary caregiver and the child develops because the child and caregiver are mentally and emotionally on the same wavelength. They share an understanding of each other's thoughts and feelings. They get a sense of what the other feels and thinks without needing to express it out loud. Their special connection helps them to understand each other well. As a result, the child sees the world through the eyes of the caregiver. They come to know they are loved, valued and good, through these mutual exchanges, which reflect empathy. On the other hand, as we will discover, the child may also learn they are unwanted, unloved and bad when those connections fail to form as they should.

Pause for thought

Our early bonds with those who looked after us shaped our perception of ourselves and the world around us. They influenced how we grew up to relate to the world and its people. Hence the use of the expression: "the apple doesn't fall far from the tree." Let's take a moment to reflect on what we have just learned, using the following questions to help direct us:

- Do you recognise parental influences in your life which shape who you are and how you respond to different situations?

- Might there be emotional responses or ways of coping you have learned from them?

- Have their struggles in dealing with life's difficulties become your struggles?

One of the best descriptions I have encountered that captures this sense of mutual exchange within the context of these early connections comes from Andrew and Rachel Wilson.

They co-authored the book, *The Life You Never Expected,* about thriving while parenting children with special needs. They describe this back and forth as being like playing attachment tennis. Rachel says this:

> I recently met someone who does training on how attachment works, and she described bonding with your child as a game of tennis. Sometimes we serve the ball into a part of the court where the child is not standing and miss them completely. They then attempt to serve to us, but the ball falls short and hits the net (She wants me to sing a song from The Lion King fifteen times in a row, and I don't.) The game has no momentum, no back and forth, and becomes frustrating for both players. What is needed is for me as the parent, to adapt my game into the one the child wants to play, however simple that is. So return the serve, stack Tupperware, read the same book back to back, hug them as they watch Peppa Pig for the millionth time. For them, that's the joy of the game.[4]

This challenge is real. Parenting requires hard work, and most people universally accept this fact. Consistently connecting with a child in a way they can engage with can exhaust a caregiver and conflict with their own needs. As a quick aside, and as a

---

4. Andrew and Rachel Wilson, *The Life You Never Expected*, (IVP, 2015), p.76.

parent of children with special needs, I will be the first to admit we do not always get this right. Knowing perfect parenting doesn't exist reassures us greatly, "good enough parenting suffices". Yet, learning to improve and finding ways to connect with your children remains essential. Understanding the importance of these early bonds enables caregivers to connect more effectively with their children.

Characteristics of our early bonds

Dr. Bowlby's work enhances our understanding. He identified four key characteristics of early bonds: secure base, safe haven, staying close and fear of being apart. Each plays a crucial role in a child's development. These four elements help us better understand the relationship's meaning and how it meets the psychological needs of the infant, particularly as they seek to discover more of the world around them:

- The notion of a **secure base** describes the connection between the caregiver and the child as a place of security, safety and support. From this base, they venture out into the world knowing they can return when needed. At a playground, for example, under the caregiver's watchful eye, the child goes off and explores but may need to check back in occasionally. A child with a strong connection to their caregiver will naturally be curious about the world beyond their early experiences and feel safe to explore. This strong connection has taught them to trust. They understand the world as a good place because they experience home as good. They generally feel confident and optimistic about life and its possibilities.

- The concept of **safe haven** refers to the role of the caregiver in providing security, comfort and stability to the child when they may be feeling overwhelmed, distressed and anxious. The child returns to the caregiver as a safe haven to experience comfort and reassurance. So, at the playground, if the child falls over and grazes their knee, they will need to come back to the caregiver for comfort and reassurance and possibly for a plaster too. Providing a safe haven plays an essential role in helping the child learn to cope with and manage their emotions. When a child cannot communicate their needs, they experience situations of high stress. In a high-stress situation, the body produces special hormones from a gland on top of the kidneys. When the needs of the child arise, causing anxiety, the level of the hormones goes up. When the caregiver meets the needs and provides comfort and reassurance, the level of the hormones goes down. Through this cycle of having their needs met and hormone levels going up and down, the child learns how to cope with and manage their emotions. They learn to feel better or more comfortable in various circumstances. When the caregiver fails to meet the needs and the level of these hormones remains elevated for significant periods, this condition becomes known as "toxic stress". Unfortunately, being stressed for a long time can stop the brain from growing the way it should and can lead to lasting problems with both mental and physical health. We will touch on the impact of this on the child in the next chapter.

- The other two characteristics go hand in hand: **staying close** and **fear of being separated**. Initially, the child stays sufficiently close to the caregiver to enable them to venture out and explore without going too far. If they get anxious about being separated from the caregiver, they know they can always return to the secure base for reassurance and comfort. This response, linked to their survival instinct, reflects a normal and healthy reaction from the child. A child's anxiety when separated from their caregiver plays a vital role in forming an emotional bond between them.

The Circle of Security

The Circle of Security (from Circle of Security International) incorporates these elements into a visual map that encourages caregivers to consider how they can provide a safe and supportive environment for their children.[5]

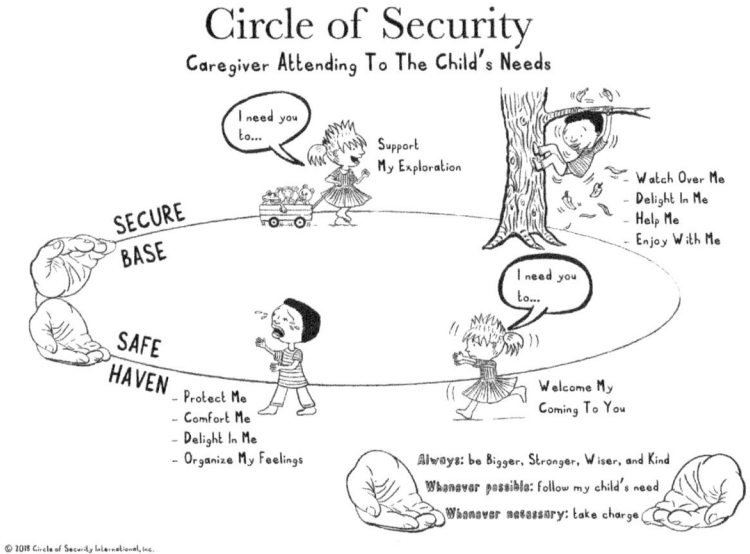

In this picture, you have two hands on one side, one representing the notion of a secure base, and the other the concept of a safe haven. The circle goes out on one side from the secure base, representing the child going out and exploring. The circle returns on the other side to the safe haven, representing the child returning to the caregiver for reassurance and comfort. The child's psychological needs vary depending on where they are in the circle. Whilst going out, the child might need you to delight in them, watch over them or enjoy

---

5. https://www.circleofsecurityinternational.com/circle-of-security-model/what-is-the-circle-of-security/

with them. When returning, they are more likely to need comfort, reassurance and help managing and controlling their feelings.

This model helps direct attention at any given time to where a child falls on the circle and, accordingly, what their psychological needs might be. This allows the caregiver to be more in tune with the child's needs, promoting better connection and increased acceptance and trust. Interestingly, the terminology used throughout this visual map appears consistently throughout the Psalms, starting with Psalm 121:8, where the psalmist tells us, "The Lord will watch over your coming and going both now and forevermore."

This appears in healthy families when caregivers engage in a dance of connection with their child and are in tune with their physical, emotional and psychological needs. The child feels connected and optimistic and holds a positive self-image. They feel loved, valued and valuable. They grow confident and eager to explore the world. They develop trusting relationships with their caregiver, which also form the basis for developing trust with others.

This all sounds positive and it's great when this happens. If you experienced this growing up, none of this would have surprised you. Your experience, however, may have been different. Some of this may have been quite alien and may have come as a surprise.

A friend of mine remembers an interaction between their godson and his mother many years ago. After disciplining him, she hugged him and told him that he was loved. This surprised my friend because it departed from their childhood experience. When these positive reciprocal interactions are missing in early childhood, this impacts what a child believes and their expectations of themselves and others. These interactions mainly determine how much trust an individual develops, along with other consequences for their mental growth.

We have considered what God's original plan looked like with healthy natural bonds forming between the caregiver and their child.

But what happens when the relationship breaks down and needs go unmet? What impact does this have on the child's development? We will explore this next as we dive deeper into understanding how much of an effect these early connections have on us.

While we often see these patterns clearly in the lives of adopted children or those who experienced early trauma, these issues aren't limited to these situations. Many of us carry wounds from relationships that didn't meet our emotional needs, whether through family dynamics, broken friendships, or life experiences that left us feeling unseen or disconnected. Even if your story doesn't involve adoption or obvious childhood struggles, these early relational patterns can still shape how you trust others—and how you connect with God.

Prayer

As the deer pants for water,
so I long for you, O God.
I thirst for God, the living God."
Psalm 42:1-2

Heavenly Father, as we begin to reflect on our connection to our earthly fathers and mothers, we acknowledge the impact they have had on our lives. We recognise how those experiences shaped our understanding of ourselves, the world and our relationship to others. We long deeply to know your presence and enjoy intimate relationship with you. Heal the wounds from our past and help us to find in you our secure base and safe haven. Empower us to explore the world and discover new possibilities, knowing that we always have a point of return and your safe hands to retreat to when we need it.

In Jesus' name, Amen.

CHAPTER 2

MISSING THE BUILDING BLOCKS OF BELONGING: INSECURE CHILDHOOD FOUNDATIONS

I've had so many conversations with my daughter, asking her to tell me the truth about something we both already know she's done. And how many times has she attempted to stubbornly flat out deny it? Not because she's a bad kid, or even because she wants to upset me. But because, for her, telling the truth feels risky. No matter how many times I tell her that it's safe to be honest with me, that she won't get in trouble just for admitting something, her brain tells her otherwise. Early on, she learned that trusting people doesn't always end well. So, in those moments, it's like survival kicks in, and she says whatever she thinks will protect her.

It's hard to describe what that feels like as a parent. Knowing she doesn't trust me, even when I've done everything I can to prove I'm safe, hurts in a way I didn't expect. Some days, she clings to me like I'm the only steady thing in her world. Other days, she pushes me away with words that sting, testing me: 'Will you still be here if I push you first?' And the answer is always yes. But knowing why she struggles doesn't make it any easier. Love isn't supposed to be this complicated. But for kids who've learned early on that love isn't always safe, trusting it can feel like the biggest risk in the world."

And it's not just kids. The more I've reflected on my daughter's struggle, the more I've realised how many of us carry the same fear. Maybe it's not as obvious. Maybe we don't lie to protect ourselves or lash out when people get too close. But deep down, many of us have learned that relationships aren't always safe. We've experienced rejection, betrayal, or neglect. And those early wounds shape how we connect with others—and even how we approach God.

Those early bonds we form with our caregivers shape our ability to trust and feel secure. What happens when those bonds don't form correctly and trust and security are broken? When the people who were supposed to make us feel safe don't (or can't) meet our emotional needs, it leaves a mark. Missing or inconsistent connections can lead to trust issues and emotional struggles, affecting how we see ourselves and relate to others. By understanding these challenges, we can find ways to rebuild and heal, creating a stronger sense of belonging and security.

Inconsistent or absent care

Not all early interactions between a caregiver and a child result in the forging of healthy early bonds and reciprocal connections. Caregivers don't always stay in tune with their children's needs as they should, sometimes providing inconsistent care or even no care at all. This may lead to Social Services involvement, who support parents to develop a connection with their child and meet their needs.

Where this is not possible and the child is sadly not able to remain with the family, they may have to seek an alternative placement through foster care and adoption. One of our adopted children was placed for adoption from birth. They lived with loving Christian foster carers for six months and then came to us as their forever family. Social Services removed the other child we adopted from the birth family and they came to us at 3.5 years old. Before being placed in a foster home, the birth family had not met their needs nor formed a healthy bond with them.

Adoption remains very much the exception. Most of us grew up with a mum and dad who looked after us as best they could, though it may not always have been good enough.

A healthy cycle of connection between a caregiver and their child consists of:

- The child experiences a need such as hunger, discomfort or pain.
- The child expresses the need through crying.
- The caregiver assesses the need and meets it.
- The child learns to trust the caregiver due to the need being met.

In the context of a healthy early bond, the caregiver met all or most of the child's needs. As adults, they enjoy relative stability and can generally cope with and manage their emotions well. These early stable foundations enable them to thrive and excel socially, emotionally and intellectually. They formed healthy early bonds and reciprocal connections with their caregivers. They develop what we refer to as a secure attachment.

When the relationship does not follow this pattern, then we have an unhealthy cycle of connection, which might look something like this:

- The child experiences a need such as hunger, discomfort, pain, or loneliness.
- The child expresses the need through crying.
- The caregiver fails to meet the need and bring relief. They neglect or ignore the child who remains in a state of discomfort.

- The child doesn't feel OK and perceives adults the same way. As a result of unmet needs, the child learns to mistrust.

- The child views the world as an unsafe place.

This will likely impact the child's beliefs and their expectations of themselves and others. They cried, expecting the caregiver to provide them with relief and comfort. The caregiver failed to meet the need. Caregivers may sometimes meet the child's needs and sometimes not. This inconsistent care creates a sense of ambivalence: the child does not know whether the caregiver will meet their needs or not. Or the caregiver consistently fails to meet the needs altogether. The child may eventually stop expressing needs since they learn that their crying serves no purpose. Insecurely attached children learn not to trust adults and see the world as an unsafe place. They lack a secure base from which to explore the world with confidence and to which they can return. They also lack any sense of a safe haven. When anxiety or distress arises, they remain unsure whether the caregiver will provide them with comfort and reassurance and help them organise their feelings.

Disrupted behaviours

A child who doesn't feel secure in their early years might develop certain behaviours which don't make much sense to us and are particularly frustrating. These can only truly be understood when we grasp the profound and lasting impact of a lack of reciprocal connection and healthy early bonds.

To give us more context within which to understand these behaviours, Sarah Naish (adoptive parents and attachment specialist) uses the analogy of a child driving a car:

> Someone put my child in the driver's seat of a car! Even worse, it was someone who should have been looking after my child. Even worse, the steering wheel was tampered with to make the car turn left when the child turned right. To make it harder, someone cut the brakes. Then, this person started the ignition and fixed the accelerator pedal down to the floor to make it speed off! My child was in the driver's seat of a car that couldn't stop, went the wrong way and was moving fast[1]

This analogy provides an excellent context for understanding what lies behind some of the behaviours we see in children who have experienced neglect, abuse and trauma in their early years. They will likely respond from a place of significantly heightened emotions, including fear, impulse, shame and anger. Put yourself in the driver's seat of that car for a minute. Picture yourself careering down the road, crashing into things, pedestrians jumping out of the way and people angrily waving their fists at you. How do you think you would feel? If this feels all too familiar, you may not have to use much imagination. Take a moment to reflect on whether you can relate to this from your own experience. Then, centre yourself for a moment and breathe before we continue further.

Many behaviours result from a caregiver failing to properly and fully meet a child's needs. We are going to cover only some of them. Together, we will briefly explore a few to illustrate what you might encounter.

Firstly, a child may struggle to understand cause and effect. For example, when a child cries to express a need (cause) and a caregiver responds to meet the need (effect), a healthy relationship forms,

---

1. Sarah Naish, *The A-Z of Therapeutic Parenting*, (Jessica Kingsley Publishers, 2018) p.18.

helping the child learn this concept. This interaction creates brain pathways which reinforce the link between cause and effect. On the other hand, an insecure, anxious child may fear trying new things, leading to fewer such pathways in the brain and slowed mental growth. If a caregiver inconsistently meets a child's needs, these pathways may not form correctly, leading to difficulties in managing emotions and understanding cause and effect. The child's sense of "why" they do something relies on these pathways, which develop through repeated experiences of expressed and met needs. These pathways provide the child with a sense of purpose or reason behind their actions.

Secondly, another consequence of unmet needs involves the child developing learned helplessness. When a child expresses discomfort or distress and receives no response from the caregiver, they may believe their actions don't matter. This feeling of helplessness can make them think there's no point in trying because nothing will change. This vicious cycle disrupts their grasp of cause and effect and slows the growth of vital brain pathways.

Thirdly, they may struggle with understanding pain and proportionality. In a healthy relationship, the child experiences pain in various forms and the caregiver helps by bringing relief. The cycle of pain and relief helps the child identify pain. In our family, as we talk about it with our children, we differentiate between little deals and big deals. When a caregiver severely neglects a child who experiences constant discomfort without relief, everything can end up being a big deal. They may scream out, although the pain amounts to just 'a little ouchy'.

These are just a few examples of the expected behaviours resulting from needs being met inconsistently or not at all. I know many adoptive families who have experienced aspects of all of these and other common behaviours resulting from neglect in the early years. In addition to behaviours and coping strategies, children also develop an 'attachment style'. In addition to the secure attachment style, there are also different types of insecure attachment. Mary Ainsworth initially developed these different attachment styles using an experiment she called *The Strange Situation*. This has become a standardised procedure for observing attachment styles in children.

Attachment styles

Ainsworth placed a child and parent in a room for a few minutes, during which time the child explored, and the parent supervised. A stranger entered the room, spoke first to the parent and then approached the child. The parent quietly left the room, leaving the child alone for a few minutes with the stranger. The parent then returned to the room and comforted the child. From her observations of the different reactions children had to the various stages of this experiment, Ainsworth concluded that three types of attachment exist: secure, anxious and avoidant. Mary Main and Dr. Judith Solomon subsequently expanded this work by adding a fourth attachment style: disorganised.

- <u>Secure</u> - The child with this attachment style showed signs of distress when the parent left the room. They tended to avoid the stranger when the parent was not present but seemed content to be friendly when the parent was there. They were cheerful and happy when the parent returned to the room. They confidently explored the room, using the parent as a secure base. The securely attached child feels connected, optimistic and holds a positive self-image. They feel loved, valued and valuable. They explore the world with confidence and eagerness.

- <u>Avoidant</u> - The child with this attachment style showed no signs of distress when the parent left the room. They were not afraid of the stranger's presence and continued to play. They also didn't pay much attention when the parent returned to the room and were comforted equally by either the parent or the stranger. Children with this attachment style often seem withdrawn, quiet and anxious. They might avoid or ignore caregivers, showing little preference between their parents and strangers. They can appear emotionally and physically independent, often keeping their distance to protect themselves from more pain and abandonment. This behaviour develops as a coping strategy, part of their survival instinct. Typically, this attachment style emerges when caregivers neglect or remain emotionally unavailable.

- <u>Ambivalent</u> - Children with this attachment style appeared highly distressed when the parent left the room. They avoided the stranger and expressed fear towards this person they did not know. They approached the parent when they returned but shied away from physical contact. They cried more and more as the experiment continued and seemed more reluctant to explore their surroundings. Children with this attachment style often seem anxious and insecure, asking a lot of questions and clinging closely to their caregiver. They can be wary of strangers and overly dependent on their caregiver, needing constant reassurance. This behaviour usually develops when caregivers are inconsistent—sometimes meeting the child's needs and others not—leaving the child unsure of what to expect.

- <u>Disorganised</u> - The child with this attachment style reacts inconsistently to the stresses of the situation. They may cry when the parent leaves the room, yet they avoid them upon their return. Or they may approach the parent but then stop in their tracks or fall to the floor. Children with this attachment style often feel angry and sad, and making friends can be challenging. They feel confused and apprehensive, unsure if they can feel safe with their caregiver. While they naturally form a relationship with their caregiver, they also fear them. This conflicted behaviour usually stems from experiencing abuse or trauma in childhood, coupled with a fearful home environment.

Pause for thought

Understanding all of this takes effort. Watching a video that explains more and includes a real-life example could be very beneficial. One of the best videos I've encountered is called *The Attachment Theory: How Childhood Affects Life*[2], produced by an organisation called Sprouts. They create cartoons that simplify complicated ideas. You might want to check out this video before reading further.

You may also have started to relate personally to how these issues played out in your childhood and your relationship with your parents. The following questions may help you to think about your attachment style as a child:

- Were you content, engaged and on task?

- Were you withdrawn, quiet and anxious?

- Were you anxious, not focussed, insecure and asking many questions?

- Were you angry, depressed, not following directions and finding it hard to make friends?

As you consider these questions, remember to be kind to yourself. The goal isn't self-judgement but reflection on how things were. This process focuses on understanding rather than criticism. Expanding your understanding should foster compassion and empathy, both essential to your healing journey.

---

2. https://www.youtube.com/watch?v=WjOowWxOXCg

Conditions of worth

Psychologist Carl Rogers used the term "conditions of worth" to describe the beliefs we form about ourselves based on how others treat us. We feel we must meet these criteria to gain acceptance, value and love. If not met, they can make us feel unworthy.

Caregivers play a vital role in this process. Children may feel secure if they receive unconditional love and acceptance. However, if love and acceptance depend on specific behaviours or achievements, or if the child sees it that way, these conditions become internalised. This shapes their beliefs about themselves and the world.

Our experiences and perceptions play a crucial role in shaping our self-worth. A caregiver may provide unconditional love, but if it seems tied to certain conditions, this belief can affect the child's understanding of their worth. For example, a caregiver might love unconditionally but also praise the child a lot for specific behaviours. This can make the child believe that love and acceptance depend on those behaviours.

As a child, I believed my value was linked to my performance and achievements. I did well in school, and my parents and teachers praised me for it. I felt like a better person when I succeeded. This drive for excellence made it hard to handle failure. I felt as though I was worth less if I failed. I also tended to take criticism personally.

Understanding the development of conditions of worth proves essential for self-acceptance. This knowledge helps us see their impact on our beliefs about ourselves and others. By recognising and challenging these internalised conditions, we can reclaim our sense of worth and embrace the intrinsic value that comes from being loved and accepted as we are.

Missing building blocks

Another way of viewing child development uses the analogy of a wall. Healthy early bonds and reciprocal connection provide solid foundational building blocks. In the first six months, these include cuddles, love, milk, comfort, warmth, stimulation, eye contact and a sense of belonging. A sensitive, understanding caregiver provides all of these things naturally. On that foundation, the child builds with additional blocks of healthy boundaries, friendships, understanding, supervision, family, speech, love and safety. Then, in the build-up to school, the child adds play, language, encouragement, love, trust, more boundaries, deeper friendships and social skills. One level of the wall builds upon the next. The building blocks mirror the pathways in the brain, which build upon already established pathways to establish further and faster connections. By building the wall in a healthy context, each layer of blocks builds naturally upon the previous solid foundation. But what happens when some of those blocks are missing?

Missing blocks in the early part of the wall leads to further missing blocks higher up as time passes. Where healthy bonds have not been formed in those early years, there has likely been a lack of stimulation and eye contact. They may not have received many cuddles. They would likely not have felt a sense of belonging. Without these foundations, they would not develop a sense of family. They may struggle to make friends. They could easily be delayed in their speech and understanding. Some of these blocks may be missing altogether. Others may be present but broken. These are insecure childhood foundations upon which building a healthy and fulfilling life may become difficult, though not impossible. Change remains possible.

Within the context of adoption, adopters are trained to look out for missing blocks in their child's wall and to seek to put those blocks in place, starting with the lower blocks and working their way up. Children who form healthy early bonds through reciprocal connection will likely form secure attachments. Their wall stands solid and healthy. We know personally of an adopted child who, having been neglected, has blocks missing. They struggled in some aspects of connection with their adoptive parents as a result. Their speech and understanding were significantly delayed. Their parents adopted them later on and they lagged in their development.

Fortunately, their brain, like yours and mine, is pretty flexible. Think of it like playdough. They may not have had the best start, but they can reshape their brain and form new pathways. This is achieved through positive experiences, therapy and reciprocal connection to their adoptive parents. Through their bond with their adoptive parents, targeted interventions at school and lots of prayer, hope exists that they will catch up and progress well in all areas. The wall slowly but surely rebuilds from the bottom up, one building block at a time.

If hope exists for them, it exists for anyone struggling with similar issues. If exploring these relational issues raises more questions than answers, don't worry healing remains possible through connection to God the Father.

Struggling to form healthy connection

Before examining how these childhood factors influence our adult lives, let's briefly address some of the reasons why caregivers and children may struggle to form healthy early bonds and reciprocal connections. Someone may bear responsibility, though that's not always the case. The different reasons include:

- When the caregiver faces an especially rough patch as the child enters the family. This could be mental difficulties such as depression or circumstantial, as in the case of a breakdown of a relationship. The caregiver may be so worried, anxious and overwhelmed that they cannot focus entirely on the child's needs. This can make the bonding process harder, and the caregiver may need to work through the issues before concentrating fully on the child's needs.

- Medical conditions in children may impact the connection process. Examples of these are things like autism, deafness, blindness and other medical conditions causing infants to cry incessantly (such as bad colic). Forming bonds is a two-way street. Some issues impact the child's creation of a healthy bond, but some impact the caregiver's doing the same. Medical conditions can make it seem as though the child doesn't respond to the care given to them. This can then impact the parents' perception of the bonding process with their children.

- Self-centred caregivers who put their own needs above those of the child. And again, bear in mind they may have not been capable of doing things differently.

- When terrible things happened to us in our childhood, making it hard to feel safe and secure, affecting how we form relationships later in life. Examples include among others: Physical abuse, sexual abuse, psychological abuse, neglect including not having enough to eat, having dirty or ill-fitting clothes, domestic violence, substance misuse or alcoholism in the home, not being made to feel unique or important, divorce or separation of caregivers, mental illness of a caregiver and incarceration of a family member.

Children develop secure attachment to loving caregivers who are in tune with them and carefully meet their physical, emotional and psychological needs. Where these early bonds were disrupted or non-existent, it can impact a child long after growing up. These early experiences echo into our adult lives. Here, we have the immediate consequences for a child of not having a secure early connection with their caregiver. Next, we will consider how this carries over into adulthood. You will start to grasp how relevant these considerations are to how securely you connect to others and what may cause you to relate to people the way you do.

Prayer

Jeremiah 30:17: "'But I will restore you to health and heal your wounds,' declares the Lord."

Heavenly Father, as you begin to show us where things may have taken a wrong turn early in our lives, would you fill us with a sense of understanding and compassion for ourselves. Be gentle with us as you uncover the insecurities of our foundations. And fill us with a sense of hope that you will bring about a work of healing and transformation in our lives.

In Jesus' name, Amen.

Chapter 3

How the Past Influences the Present: The Mirror of Adulthood

While there were moments in my childhood where I felt connected—like in the kitchen with my mum—there were just as many times where I felt alone, misunderstood, or like I didn't quite belong. No matter what I achieved, I'd hear this voice in the back of my mind: 'Any minute now, they're going to realise you're not good enough.' I struggled to believe I belonged anywhere—whether in friendships, at work, or even in my relationship with God.

I knew the right things to say, the right things to believe. But deep down, I wrestled with the fear that I wasn't enough. That somehow, I was disqualified from the kind of love and connection others seemed to experience so easily. It wasn't until I began to see how these feelings were tied to my early experiences—times when I felt misunderstood, unseen, or like I didn't fit—that I started to understand how deeply my past was influencing my present.

Our early relationships shape us in ways we don't always realise. They affect how we view ourselves, how we trust others and how we navigate the world. The bonds we form with our caregivers teach us whether our needs will be met—or ignored. They help us learn whether it's safe to open up or better to stay guarded. And these lessons don't stay in childhood. They follow us into adulthood, shaping our friendships, our marriages and even our relationship with God.

Take Sarah, for instance. She grew up in a home where affection was rare and emotions were often dismissed. When she was upset, her parents would tell her to "toughen up" or that she was "too sensitive." Over time, Sarah learned to hide her feelings and stopped expecting comfort from others. As an adult, she found it hard to trust people, constantly fearing that if she opened up, she'd be rejected or judged. This same fear spilled over into her spiritual life. She believed God loved her in a general sense but struggled to feel it personally.

Adult attachment styles

The same four childhood attachment styles are reflected in our adult styles of attachment.

- **Secure attachment**: Children who form healthy early bonds and reciprocal connection with their caregivers grow up with a generally positive view of themselves and their relationships. As adults, they feel comfortable with closeness and can depend on others appropriately. They typically handle stress well and communicate openly. They tend to form stable, long-lasting relationships. They might feel comfortable sharing their thoughts and feelings with a close friend or family member. They manage conflict well and respond accordingly to other people's needs. They tend to take more risks and actively pursue personal growth. They have a greater chance of developing into the best version of themselves. They will grow up to use their talents and skills to do things that make them happy and fulfilled. They will use what they have to do good to themselves and to others. They have a greater awareness of what makes them special and use it to live a happy and meaningful life. This attachment style, known as secure, fosters stability. Joseph represents an example from the Bible of a character who may be considered to have a secure attachment style. Many of the positive aspects of his journey and his resilience in the face of adversity can be linked to his strong relationship with his father, Jacob.

- **Avoidant attachment**: Neglected children who rarely had their needs met, grow up tending to maintain emotional distance from others. As adults, they value their independence and self-sufficiency highly, often seeming distant. They may want connection but struggle to trust others fully or get too emotionally close. They might struggle with conflicting feelings about closeness and are less likely to seek or offer support during stressful situations. Their relationships might lack depth due to their hesitance to open up emotionally. The biblical character of Jonah could be said to show traits of someone with an avoidant attachment style. He tended to withdraw from relationships. He isolated himself on several occasions, literally trying to run in the opposite direction. His emotional responses lacked empathy and compassion.

- **Anxious attachment**: Children who were never sure whether their needs would be met (due to inconsistent care) often grow up feeling less secure in their relationships. As adults, they may need constant reassurance and affection from those around them, such as friends, family members, or colleagues. Anxiously attached individuals may seek constant validation from their friends and struggle with feelings of insecurity in social situations. They may appear clingy or overly dependent on others for emotional support. Their relationships can sometimes face challenges due to their high need for closeness and approval. King Saul, from the Bible, may have shown traits of this kind of attachment style. He appeared to need constant reassurance from those around him. He felt insecure about the prospect of the kingdom being taken away from him. He did not fully trust Samuel to come and decided to offer the sacrifice on the altar himself rather than wait. And in his relationship with David, he went back and forth constantly between expressing affection and attempting to kill him.

- **Disorganised attachment**: Abused children who lived in fear growing up, lack a clear strategy for emotional attachments and relationships. As adults with a disorganised attachment style, they often exhibit erratic behaviour and mixed signals which can confuse others. Their relationships often fluctuate, marked by highs and lows. These individuals might struggle with trust issues, fear of rejection, or difficulties forming close connections. Samson, a complicated character, may have had traits of this attachment style. At times, he came across as very impulsive, and at other times, he appeared to be seeking closeness in his relationships. He lived a life of chaos and disorder, which ultimately led to a tragic death.

Using tools of modern-day psychology to interpret biblical characters may be considered by some to be unconventional. I am not seeking to diagnose or make definitive statements. However, observing how these traits manifest to varying degrees in their lives can point us to an alignment between attachment theory and biblical narratives.

> **Pause for thought**
>
> Take a moment to think about your attachment style and how it relates to your early life experiences.
>
> - Do you relate to any of one of these styles in particular?
>
> - If you can see links between who you are now and what it was like growing up, does that understanding help to put things into perspective?
>
> These might be difficult questions if they are things you have not considered before or have not thought about for a long time. If they are, then check in with yourself. Take a breath. If you need to, talk to someone else about your feelings. And take a moment to give these things to God before you continue.

My own struggles with connection

At this point, I would like to share with you something of my own story. I grew up in a Christian home and came to faith at age seven, standing in front of a mirror. Accepting Christ into my life probably took at most thirty-five seconds. Accepting me took the best part of the next thirty-five years. My experience of life growing up could have been better. Alongside those times of connection with my family, I also remember being constantly bullied and left out for being different. Severe and prolonged bullying qualifies as one of those terrible things that happens to children. I had very few friends. I did not get on with my brother at all. We spent more time fighting than anything else.

My recollection of my relationship with my parents is really complicated and somewhat confusing. They were there for me. There were amazing times of connection as previously mentioned that have shaped me into who I am today in really positive ways. They met all of my obvious needs. Dad did all the things dads are supposed to do. He was present and engaged and dare I say devoted as far as I can recall. Yet it never felt like he got me or understood me, and he wasn't especially emotionally available. Growing up, it felt like no one got me. This was a lonely place to be. Being a Christian didn't make much difference, especially since I didn't have friends at church either.

If you go back to picturing the wall, most of my building blocks were in place, but a few were missing: belonging, friendship and social skills. I grew up in a loving family where they met my needs as best they knew how. I still developed relational insecurities and a somewhat ambivalent attachment style as a result of not having a sense of belonging and not having friends. At University, I continued desperately to try and find my place in the world, longing for acceptance and belonging, so I tried to fit in. This didn't help because I attempted to mould to what I thought others wanted of me instead of expressing my own personality. Trying to fit in just brought more isolation and loneliness.

After University, I worked for a Christian lawyer and participated in a local church. I had a good job and a good church. Life was OK, but I still felt lonely and ended up in counselling as a result. I just wanted to do life with someone who could get me and love me for who I was. Not long after that, I met my wife, and guess what? She didn't get me either. Both our attachment styles and relational insecurities carried over into our intimate relationship too.

Love languages

In his 1992 book *The Five Love Languages*, Dr. Gary Chapman said people show and feel love in five main ways: words of affirmation, acts of service, receiving gifts, quality time and physical touch. He wanted to help people understand what makes them or others feel loved so they can show love in the best way. Understanding love languages can create stronger connections and intimacy. Love languages play a big role in romantic relationships and with parents, children, friends and co-workers.

We have established how our early bonds with caregivers shape how we see ourselves and the world. They also affect how we meet our emotional needs in relationships. How caregivers show love affects how we receive love as adults. Therefore, understanding love languages can improve emotional connections. For example, someone with an anxious attachment style might need constant reassurance through words of affirmation. Someone with an avoidant attachment style might avoid physical touch or quality time.

The way an individual behaves doesn't necessarily reflect their true personality. It may reflect a learned behaviour. A caregiver who emphasises gifts might lead a child to link love with presents. However, the child might naturally prefer love through physical touch. This dynamic pulls them between who they are and who they've been taught to be, making it harder to feel genuinely connected.

Reflecting on these dynamics can help us reassess our needs and align our love languages with our authentic selves, leading to deeper and more satisfying connections. We will return to this later.

Terrible things that happened in childhood

Childhood experiences deeply impact us. My childhood offered a mixed bag—some aspects were really good, others not so great. This might be true for many people. However, some grew up with no sense of safety or security. You might relate to this. The consequences of this in later life are often far-reaching. Over the years, I have worked with people who have faced many kinds of hardship. Not long after we moved to Wolverhampton, my wife and I ran a dedicated homegroup for heroin addicts, alcoholics, people struggling with mental health issues and people experiencing transitionary periods of homelessness. Everyone who came to our group had been in care as a result of relational wounds and insecurities. They all had multiple instances of terrible things happening to them as a child. These are called ACEs (which stands for adverse childhood experience). Research suggests that 90% of people experiencing homelessness have at least one ACE, and 54% have four or more.[1]

We learnt a lot from this group. Much of it broke our hearts. They were all convinced they were unwanted, unloved and bad. This stands in contrast to what a child learns when they forge healthy early bonds with their caregivers. Their negative views of themselves permeated their thinking deeply. The gospel could not apply to them because they were in a special category of really bad people God could not save. Whilst we know that this is not true, their feelings linked directly to the terrible things that had happened to them in their childhood.

Dave was so convinced he was rotten to the core, he barely dared set foot in church. We had to use fruity language to help him think about things differently. We used to tell him: *"God loves f***** up a***holes like you and me."* I am sorry if this language offends you;

---

1. Lancet Public Health Journal, https://doi.org/10.1016/S2468-2667(21)00210-3

however, it was necessary under the circumstances. We had to use language relevant to him because of how he viewed himself. This left no room for him to exclude himself. The Bible clearly states, "all have sinned and fallen short of the glory of God" (Romans 3:23). We all need God's redemption and grace through Jesus Christ. This way of explaining it helped him understand how grace also applied to him. I think it blew his mind. I was suggesting I was no different to him and this particular phrase was as relevant to me as it was to him.

Working with this group, we learned we had to love them first before we tried to convince them Jesus loved them. They were convinced they were unlovable, unwanted and bad. So, the thought anyone could love them, Jesus included, was utterly alien to them. Those pathways in their brain related to love and connection with others had yet to be built. And the lie they were unlovable, unwanted and bad stood in the way like a giant roadblock, with a diversion sign hanging in front of it. Before we could move forward, we needed to demolish the roadblock, clear away the rubble and then help them build the pathway in their brain which would allow them to believe they could be loved by us and, in turn, by Jesus. This was a massive ask! Yet God is good and the God of the impossible. He saved lots of them, and a good few are already in heaven, living the good life they never had on this earth.

Flexibility of our brains

We can experience this kind of radical transformation because of the flexibility of our brains. For a while, professionals believed this kind of change was very hard, if not impossible. People thought that once the brain had been wired in a particular way, you were stuck with it. A book recommended to us during adoption training ten years ago claimed the brain couldn't change after a certain age. The adoption trainer sought to highlight the importance of those early connections and getting it right the first time.

This belief did not sit well with us then, mainly because of two words: But God. And also because the Apostle Paul commands us to: "be transformed by the renewing of your minds" (Romans 12:2). Scripture explicitly confirms that our brains can be transformed and we can change how we think. Scientists now know the brain can evolve and change over time. I love that as science discovers, evolves and learns, it brings us closer to our understanding of God.

Most people now accept that the brain can be rewired. We can have a bad start in life, end up with all sorts of issues as a result, and yet become more secure in our relationships and connections to others in later life. We can develop a new attachment style called 'earned secure attachment'.

Earned secure attachment

Whether our difficulties forming healthy connections come from adoption, family dynamics, or life's challenges, the good news is that healing is possible. Earned secure attachment isn't just for adoptees—it's for anyone who's experienced broken trust and is seeking deeper, healthier connections with others and with God.

It refers to adults who have developed a secure attachment style in adulthood despite having insecure early bonds in childhood. This adjustment typically results from significant personal reflection, therapy, or meaningful relationships that offer new models of trust and intimacy. Individuals with earned secure attachment have worked through their relational wounds and insecurities, learning to form healthy, stable relationships. They show signs of feeling safe and secure, like feeling comfortable with being close to others and doing things independently. They can tell others what they need. They understand others and help those around them.

I can think of at least one relationship that offers a new model of trust and intimacy: "Whoever dwells in the shelter of the Most High will rest in the shadow of the Almighty. I will say of the Lord, 'He is my refuge and my fortress, my God, in whom I trust'" (Psalm 91:1-2). We have every reason to hope for change. Our relationship with God lies at the heart of transformation. We will explore this further when we seek to unveil the Father's heart in our relationships.

Erosion of social networks

Before we get there, we have a few more things to consider regarding how our past influences our present. We have thought about how our attachment style impacts our relationships. Unsurprisingly we can suffer social consequences when we have experienced early relational wounds or when terrible things have happened to us as children. If we struggle in our relationships, we may find it challenging to maintain them over time, and we may struggle to build new ones. This can lead to an erosion of our social networks, which get smaller and smaller with time.

I was talking this through with a close friend who recently came across the concept. They recognised this was a factor in their own life but asserted it did not matter much to them since they were a "bit of a hermit". This depicts another excellent example of what we discussed earlier regarding roadblocks on the pathway. In this example, we must ask whether my friend truly is a hermit. In their thinking, they encountered the roadblock of confronting the erosion of their social networks. Their brain then decided to form a new pathway around this roadblock, convincing them they were a hermit, so it didn't matter. In reality, my friend may be somewhat of a hermit—I'm not sure. Or maybe not. But thinking through these issues helps us understand how the brain works and how it forms new pathways to avoid obstacles.

Pause for thought

You may not have previously realised that your brain could tell you false things about yourself to protect itself from further harm and avoid having to confront issues. Self-preservation or survival instinct comes naturally to our minds. Sometimes, our brains try to protect us from what they see as potentially harmful thinking.

I have personally experienced roadblocks in my own thinking. I used to think nobody got me and everyone was out to get me. These lies prevented me from believing it is OK to be me and accepting me for who I am. We will consider later how those lies were exposed and a new way of thinking came about in my mind.

- Are there stories or narratives you tell yourself about yourself which may not be true?
- How does that make you feel?
- Might it help to ask a trusted friend or loved one to help you think through your thoughts about yourself and identify some they disagree with?

The impact on physical health

Finally, concerning the influences of the past on the present, we should briefly consider the physical complications potentially linked to relational wounds and terrible things that happened to us as children. In 1998, Dr Vince Fellitti and Dr Bob Anda carried out a medical study of 17,500 people[2]. The study asked the participants to indicate what terrible things had happened to them when they were children. A point was given for each terrible thing that happened and added up to give each participant a total score. They then cross-referenced the scores for each participant with several health outcomes in later life. The findings of the study were remarkable. This medical study concluded they had "found a strong graded relationship between the breadth of exposure to abuse or household dysfunction during childhood and multiple risk factors for several of the leading causes of death in adults." In essence, it demonstrated the more terrible things a child experienced, the more likely they were to be as an adult, at high risk for heart disease, cancer, stroke, type 2 diabetes, chronic bronchitis, fractures, hepatitis and poor self-rated health.

One particular example of relates to a family friend. Where a person obtained a score of four or more, they were 2.5 times more likely to develop chronic obstructive pulmonary disease (COPD) than someone who had a score of zero. Here, the practice meets the theory. In an evaluation against the study's criteria, my friend obtains a score of more than four. In 2019, following a persistent chest infection, they were eventually diagnosed with asthma and chronic bronchitis, one of the main conditions of COPD. We cannot definitively deduce

---

2. Vincent J. Felitti et al., "Relationship of Childhood Abuse and Household Dysfunction to Many of the Leading Causes of Death in Adults. The Adverse Childhood Experiences (ACE) Study," *American Journal of Preventive Medicine* 14, no. 4 (1998): 245-258, https://doi.org/10.1016/s0749-3797(98)00017-8.

a link between the two, but their life circumstances align with the study's findings in a pronounced way.

The early bonds we forge have a widespread impact on our childhood, our perception of the world, our view of ourselves and how these patterns carry over into adulthood. Unsurprisingly, these early bonds also impact how we parent. We tend to parent in the way we were parented, meaning that the cycle of attachment, whether secure or insecure, risks carrying over from generation to generation. What I have learned about how our early connections impact our parenting styles has changed how I approach connecting with my children.

Prayer

"Lord, you are the God who saves me;
day and night I cry out to you.
May my prayer come before you;
turn your ear to my cry."
Psalm 88:1-2

Heavenly Father, as we grow in our knowledge of how our past may still deeply impact our present, we turn to you and cry out to you. Where these thoughts may seek to overwhelm us, may you protect us, comfort us and bring us inner peace. Please help us organise our feelings and see a pathway towards restoration, secure attachment and healing through connection to you.

In Jesus name, Amen.

Chapter 4

Breaking the Chains: Transforming Generational Patterns of Connection

I've read all the books. We've gone through the training. I know the theories, the strategies, the 'right' ways to build healthy connections with my kids. But despite all of that, when I'm tired and frustrated, it all seems to go out the window.

Last night, we were watching a film together as a family, and he kept interrupting to ask questions every five minutes. But he was speaking so quietly that I couldn't hear a word he said. I had to pause the film every single time, asking him to repeat himself. Eventually, my frustration boiled over, and I shouted at him to raise his voice and speak clearly. He cried. He was shaking. I could see the walls going up. He told me he was doing his best and that I shouldn't be so hard on him.

In that moment, I wasn't just a parent trying to handle a bad day—I was reflecting the anger and frustration I'd experienced growing up, the very patterns I've tried so desperately hard to leave behind.

I'd told myself I would parent differently—more patiently, more gently. But I'm reminded in those moments that I don't always draw from the books I've read or the knowledge I've accumulated. I react from somewhere deeper, somewhere shaped by the way I was parented. And that's when it hits me again: breaking generational patterns isn't just about knowing what to do. It's about recognising how much of our past still shows up in the present.

Parenting doesn't just teach us about our children. It holds up a mirror to ourselves, exposing the patterns we've inherited from our own families—patterns of connection, disconnection, trust and fear. And unless we're paying attention, those patterns can quietly pass from one generation to the next, shaping not just how we parent, but how we relate to others and to God.

Our early attachments shape our adult relationships, impacting everything from trust to emotional well-being. The way we were parented influences how we parent, how we connect with our children, and how we relate to the world. By understanding these generational patterns, we can learn to break the chains of negative cycles and create healthier, more secure connections for future generations.

Different types of father

Jon Tyson (Senior pastor at Church of the City of New York) and Jeff Bethke (New York Times best-selling author) did a series of podcasts together called *Intentional Family*. In this series, they explored what has gone wrong with family, fatherhood and parenting in general and what it might look like to do things differently as Christians. As a parent, I have greatly benefitted from listening to their discussions and recommend you consider checking it out if you are at this stage of life yourself.

In the first episode, entitled *What's Gone Wrong with Fatherhood,*[1] Jon Tyson distinguishes between five different types of fathers:

- The "irresponsible father" serves as effectively nothing more than a sperm donor

- The "ignorant father" just doesn't have a clue about parenting or how to bring up a child, let alone a securely attached one.

- The "inconsistent father" goes back and forth between presence and absence. This may be because their career or personal aspirations compete with their role as a parent.

- The "involved father" appears to do everything right. They show up, remain present and dedicate themselves to the task. They engage fully in their child's life, covering all the bases. This already works well, yet they could still do more.

- The "intentional father" gets his child. They understand the child's personality and individuality and intentionally set out to help them become who God has made them to be. Scripture portrays God as the ultimate loving father, intentional in all his ways toward us—the perfect parent. In Psalm 139:16, David says, "All the days ordained for me were written in your book before one of them came to be."

The "intentional father" understands how parenting centres around connection. Parenting involves connecting with the child as an individual; meeting all of their needs purposefully and specifically; and building those healthy early bonds which will help set a child on the right path for life.

---

1. https://intentionalfamily.libsyn.com/1-whats-gone-wrong-with-fatherhood#

In an interview with Parent Circle, Dr Laura Markham, Clinical Psychologist at Columbia University, said this:

> Connection is 80% of parenting. Until we have a relationship with our children and they trust us, they won't do what we say. So, if you want your child to cooperate without threats, punishment, or bribes (or yelling at them), you need a relationship of closeness and trust, wherein your child wants to do what you say, wants to follow your lead, and doesn't want to disappoint you because she loves you and is close to you. And that's the connection. Guidance and coaching are only 20% of parenting, at best.[2]

Pause for thought

Think back to your relationship with your parents.

- How present were they?
- How involved were they?
- How well did they connect with you as an individual?

These are essential considerations since, as we will see, how we were parented often heavily influences how we parent.

---

2. https://www.parentcircle.com/how-to-connect-with-a-child-dr-laura-markham/article

Attachment styles of the fathers

There may be parallels between Jon Tyson's categorisation of different types of father and the different adult attachment styles:

- The "ignorant father" may have traits of an avoidant attachment style. Lacking any understanding of how to parent, they likely remain emotionally unavailable and disconnected. They often fail to offer support to the child simply because they don't know how. They do not know what the child's needs are or how to meet them. In the absence of having their needs met, the child may grow up to have an avoidant attachment style themselves.

- The "inconsistent father" may have traits of an anxious attachment style. They may only sometimes meet their child's needs since they have competing demands on their time and availability. These competing interests, such as personal ambition or career, may tie in with their need for affirmation and validation, which they get through performing well in a work setting. When present, they may seek to overly involve themselves to make up for their prior absence and come across as overbearing. This can lead to the child developing an anxious attachment style for themselves.

- The "involved father" presents and supports their child in a way that may show traits of secure attachment. They form healthy relationships with their children. They consistently offer support and provide for their children's needs. They manage conflict well, are emotionally available and have appropriate boundaries in their relationship with their children. Their children can explore the world with dad there, enjoying with them and available for comfort and reassurance.

- The "intentional father" takes this to a whole new level. They connect with their child and seek purposefully to plan and enhance their development. They communicate openly, validate the child's feelings and support the child's aims and goals. They adeptly meet their child's emotional, physical and psychological needs. This level of intentionality and connection within their relationship likely requires them to be securely attached themselves or to have developed an earned secure attachment at some point along the way.

Much of the focus here has been on fathers, as we have reflected on how human fathers reflect God the Father. However, we must also recognise how mothers, including single mothers, play an equally vital role in shaping relational connections and nurturing their children's emotional and spiritual growth.

Parenting from one generation to the next

These are generalisations and not definitive diagnoses, but they may help understand how the way we were parented and our attachment styles may impact how we go on to parent our children, thereby continuing the cycle into the next generation. George Hegel, a 19th-century German philosopher, famously said, "The only thing we learn from history is that we do not learn from history." This rather pessimistic way of viewing the world suggests we are somewhat doomed to keep repeating the same mistakes.

This often holds true in parenting. We may continue to do things as we were taught, which has the comfort of being familiar. Or we may react or even overreact to the way we were parented and resolve to do things differently as we set out not to make the mistakes our parents made. You may have found yourself thinking that you definitely do not want to emulate your parents and set out intentionally to compensate for their shortcomings. A child growing up in a home with many arguments may become argumentative. Or they may become someone who strives to keep the peace at all costs, even if it means they don't tend to stand up for themselves. Likewise, a child of controlling parents may become controlling or end up fiercely guarding their independence.

The quality of our relationship with our parents, or lack thereof, significantly impacts how we behave as parents. This then affects the quality of our relationship with our children. Our insecurities may become their insecurities and the cycle continues. We are not seeking to assign blame or fault. From how we were parented, we may consider retaining things we liked and felt good and rejecting things that did not sit well with us. This could relate to feelings, thoughts or behaviours.

We won't always get this right. In Romans 7:15, the Apostle Paul says: "For what I want to do I do not do, but what I hate I do." This can also be so true of us, especially at the most stressful or painful times. Sometimes, we get stressed out or strongly react to something difficult from our past. We then return to what feels most familiar and do the same things our parents did which we vowed never to replicate. In those moments, we must remind ourselves once again: we do not need to be perfect parents. We can settle for good enough parenting. These moments allow us to model asking for and receiving forgiveness, an essential part of the gospel message.

A third way our parents continue to influence us happens when we subconsciously seek to recreate familiar patterns and environments from childhood. We may replicate harmful patterns because they feel predictable. For example, a child who grew up in a home with emotionally absent caregivers may, as an adult, subconsciously choose emotionally distant partners. Or we may subconsciously act towards others in a way intended for them to behave towards us as our parents did. These efforts to recreate familiar circumstances can serve as a way for individuals to seek resolution or control over unresolved issues from their childhood. Recognising these patterns can put us on the path to breaking the cycle and creating healthier behaviours and relationships.

Biblical examples of generational parenting

The Bible also highlights generational patterns, as seen in the lives of Abraham, Isaac and Jacob. These stories show how faith, trust and relational dynamics pass down through generations (Genesis 12-50). One such example involves favouritism. While the Bible doesn't condemn the patriarchs for showing favouritism, Scripture still emphasises its significant impact on family dynamics.

For three generations, favouring one son over another led to bitterness, resentment and families torn apart:

- Sarah favoured Isaac, who was the child of the promise, over Ishmael, who was born to their maidservant Hagar. This led to the family being divided and Hagar being sent away from the family. God told Hagar in Genesis 16:12 that there would be significant conflict between the two brothers.

- Isaac continued the pattern in his treatment of his sons. Esau was his favourite. Jacob, his second son, was the favourite of their mother, Rebekah. This led to strife and division, with Rebekah helping Jacob deceive their father and brother. This drove a wedge between the two brothers.

- And again, in the next generation, Jacob has a favourite, Joseph. Genesis 37:3 tells us he "loved Joseph more than all of his children because he was the son of his old age." This favouritism, compounded by Joseph's unwise recounting of his dreams, led his brothers to resent him and sell him into slavery.

Interestingly in this last part of the narrative favouritism appears to be both the cause and the solution to the problem. We will return to this in more detail later when we consider Joseph's traits of attachment. They are closely linked to his strong relationship with his father. The impact this had on his life, the life of the family and ultimately, the nation of Israel was significant.

The sense of self

The child-caregiver relationship shapes beliefs and expectations. Children tend to internalise their early experiences. Those first impressions form lasting patterns in how they view themselves and the world around them.

However, these are only sometimes consistent with their personality and it may be hard to determine the difference between them. Many do not grow up with a fully developed sense of self. We find it hard to separate our thoughts, feelings and beliefs from those of the people we are in close relationships with, especially our parents. You may have asked yourself the question at times as to whether you understand yourself as an individual and what you think, feel and believe when setting aside the influence of others, particularly parents.

Becoming a true reflection of yourself involves developing a sense of self while maintaining an emotional connection with others. Self-discovery involves finding a balance where you can keep a healthy relationship with others, even when there are differences in opinion or feelings, without cutting them off or being overly dependent. Self-discovery contributes significantly to healthy psychological development and involves establishing personal beliefs, values, emotional regulation and life goals independent of parental influences.

To some extent, "involved parents" and, to a greater degree, "intentional parents" assist in the process. They seek to connect with us intentionally so as to develop our personality and unique giftings. They encourage and empower us to become who God created us to be.

Parents living out of their own insecurities tend to make this process much more complicated for their children. Maintaining healthy relationships may be a struggle if you have an insecure attachment style. If you have an avoidant attachment style, you will likely cut people off. If you have an anxious attachment style, you will likely be overly dependent. All this makes it much harder to be yourself while engaging meaningfully with others.

Yet, you must realise some of the behaviours, attitudes and responses you have developed over time result from past experiences, influences and coping strategies. Somewhere under the layers of the onion lies your true and unique personality. If your parents were not actively helping you be yourself, then it may take substantial work and self-seeking to peel back the layers of the onion and connect with your authentic identity.

Pause for thought

Take a moment to reflect on what it means to be you. Consider journaling, praying, or meditating on how your early relationships with those closest to you have impacted your personality.

- Do you have a strong and clear sense of who you are?

- Do you know what you like and dislike and are confident in expressing those things?

- Or are there things you sense have been imposed on you and don't sit right?

No right or wrong answers exist for these questions. They invite you on a journey of self-discovery. This process may not always be easy, but there's nothing to fear, as the Bible reminds us that we are 'fearfully and wonderfully made' (Psalm 139:14). In time, you might want to spend more time reflecting on these things—you may surprise yourself.

Struggles linked to a lack of sense of self

Without a developed sense of self and an understanding of identity, an individual may struggle with boundaries, autonomy and healthy relationships. Not feeling comfortable in their own skin may lead to several emotional, psychological and interpersonal difficulties, including:

- Difficulties in setting personal boundaries, causing them to be overly dependent or distant relationally. This can lead to being overwhelmed on the one hand or lonely on the other.

- Being easily influenced by others' feelings. The lack of a clear understanding of their own feelings can result in struggles with emotional regulation and conflict.

- Avoidance of conflict as a result of a fear of disagreements. This can cause issues in communication and leave unresolved issues and resentment.

- Heavy reliance on others for affirmation, which can cause anxiety and depression.

- Difficulty making decisions and expressing needs, which may result in confusion, dissatisfaction and a lack of purpose and direction in life.

You may have noticed the similarities between these difficulties and those associated with insecure attachment. This connection makes sense because a positive self-image proves crucial for secure attachment. In contrast, a negative self-image or lack of self-understanding typically characterises insecure attachment.

Therefore, developing a sense of self and true identity becomes essential for earning secure attachment. In other words, recognizing that it's OK to be yourself is crucial for forming healthy connections with others.

Establishing authentic identity

There are some practical steps you can take to begin to establish an authentic identity rooted in personal beliefs, values, emotional regulation and life goals:

- <u>Regular self-reflection</u> provides insight into your emotions, triggers and needs. Journaling, meditation, or mindfulness can help too. Self-reflection involves examining your feelings, reactions and psychological or emotional needs in specific situations. King David invites God into this process of self-reflection when he says, "Search me, God, and know my heart; test me and know my anxious thoughts" (Psalm 139:23).

- <u>Practise the pause</u> (as we call it in our family). This involves pausing before reacting instinctively to a situation. Take a moment to centre yourself. Then, think through your options and how you want to respond, considering your beliefs, values and emotions first. Stephen Covey (who wrote *Seven Habits of Highly Effective People*) popularised a quote he does not claim to have authored himself, which says, "In the space between stimulus (what happens) and how we respond lies our freedom to choose." Great freedom comes through pausing before responding in a manner aligned with your true self. And wisdom, too - "Wise people think before they act" (Proverbs 13:16, NLT).

- <u>Develop better communication skills</u> - This involves listening to others while clearly expressing your needs. It fosters healthy relationships and requires you to establish clear boundaries.

- <u>Look after yourself</u>, commonly known as TLC (tender loving care). Many people underestimate the importance of seeking to promote your own sense of well-being. This involves working out things which bring you joy and doing them more. Doing more of what you love can deepen your understanding of yourself. Scripture encourages us to be filled with joy in several places (such as Philippians 4:4, Proverbs 17:22)

- <u>Surround yourself with radiators:</u> You may have previously heard the famous quote about people being either drains or radiators. We are not sure who first said this, but the sense of the quote seems clear. Some people exude warmth, encouragement and good cheer, giving off positive energy. They are radiators. Others are cold, miserable and seem to have a way to suck the life, energy and positivity out of you. If you need to go on a journey of self-discovery, people who respect your boundaries and support your growth make the best companions along the way. You can build healthy relationships with these people who will encourage and empower you to be yourself. The Bible encourages us to surround ourselves with like-minded believers when it says, "Therefore encourage one another and build each other up, just as in fact you are doing" (1 Thess 5:11). Scripture also encourages us to "walk with the wise and become wise" (Proverbs 13:20).

- <u>Be accountable</u>: I love the word accountability because of how you can break it down into two words. Rather than carrying the negative connotations so often associated with this term, accountability remains fundamentally positive: an account of your ability. People who hold you to account in the true sense of the word encourage you to be yourself and to grow into being everything God created you to be and doing what he has called you to do. For example, the parable of the talents expresses this sense of the term accountability (Matthew 25:14-30 - the servants are made to account for their ability to faithfully manage what the master had given them).

- <u>Develop an attitude of gratitude</u>: Thankfulness helps you to think about what you are grateful for. This, in turn, makes you think about what makes you grateful, giving you a sense of value and what really matters to you. Thankfulness also enhances the positive emotions of joy, contentment and appreciation, all of which assist with emotional regulation. This can help to emphasise the healthy relationships in your life.

  Often, we are most grateful for the people in our lives. Thankfulness for people brings with it a sense of connection and connectedness. And if you can get to a place of being thankful for who you are and who God created you to be, then you are well on your way to learning that it is very good to be you. The Bible encourages us to "give thanks in all circumstances" (1 Thessalonians 5:18).

- <u>Seek professional help</u>: While all of the above can be helpful, sometimes an outside voice of reason and guidance should also be considered. Professional guidance in the form of counselling or therapy may be a necessary step in discovering your true self. They have tools that can help and may be useful to this journey.

These are some constructive ways of discovering our identity and, in doing so, connecting to others in healthy relationships. We can see significant change in our lives through personal reflection, engaging in therapy, or nurturing meaningful relationships that offer new models of trust and intimacy. One particular relationship I have discovered through personal experience, transforms more in this sense than any other: my relationship with God. Relationship with God has the greatest potential to model and mend the very essence of connection and love. Unveiling the Father's heart in relationships comes through applying what we have learnt thus far. We can know connection to a loving heavenly father and, in doing so, move towards healing through connection to him.

Prayer

Exodus 20:6: "But showing love to a thousand generations of those who love me and keep my commandments."

Heavenly Father, we bring before you the patterns of insecurity and brokenness that have been passed down through generations. We ask for your divine intervention to break these chains and to bring about transformation in our lives. Fill us with your strength and wisdom to create new patterns of security and trust rooted in your love. Heal our relationships and let our connections reflect your grace and compassion. May we be agents of change and see your healing power at work in our families and communities.

In Jesus' name, Amen.

Part II: Unveiling the Father's heart in relationships

His Publishing Services Ltd

Chapter 5

Knowing Connection to a Loving Heavenly Father

So far, we have focussed mainly on understanding the nature of the relationship between a child and their primary caregiver. We have considered how much of those relationships carries over into adulthood and impacts how we go on to parent. You may have wondered when we would get to explore how we can experience healing through connection with the Father. The picture will now become clearer as to what being connected to the Father means and how the sense of reciprocal connection can be applied to our relationship with God.

The Bible centres on connection

We began by looking at the dance of connection described by Dan Hughes and how that compares to the description of God rejoicing over us with singing. We also thought about how the Bible begins in Genesis and ends in Revelation with connection to God as central to the narrative. These bookends reveal the story's central theme. Just as parenting revolves around connection, so does the Bible.

I love using the Discovery Bible Study tools (DBS) when studying a passage of scripture. DBS invites you to consider four questions concerning any passage: 1) What does it say about God? 2) What does it say about people? 3) What should I do differently as a result?

and 4) Who can I share it with? The first two questions are pretty telling regarding our understanding of scripture.

Firstly, the Bible centres around its author and main character, God. Scripture begins with him, before the beginning of time: "In the beginning, God..." (Genesis 1:1). And it finishes with him as well, depicting his presence in the city of God forever. Scripture also gives a significant role to people. In the beginning, God made mankind. In the end, Revelation 22:3 references his servants who will serve him in his city. At the heart of the biblical story lies the relationship between God and people, a theme woven throughout.

At the start, the relationship was great. Then, it all fell apart when Adam and Eve sinned, and God sent them out of the Garden of Eden. The rest of the story describes how God sets about redeeming and restoring his people through the life, death and resurrection of his son, Jesus Christ. Jesus describes himself as the only way through which we can be brought back into connection with the Father: "No one comes to the Father except through me" (John 14:6). Redemption and restoration are about God rescuing us, making us whole again (healing us), and restoring our connection to him through his son Jesus. Both healing and connection to God remain central themes of the narrative of Scripture.

Insights from our earthly relationships may help us to gain valuable understanding as to how we can deepen our connection to God. The specific relationships we have been exploring thus far are between a primary caregiver and their child. If God acts as the primary caregiver in the Bible, then there may be some parallels between those earthly relationships and our relationship with him. We can loosely use the questions from the Discovery Bible Study to assist us in this process:

1. What does the Bible say about God as primary caregiver? and

2. What does the Bible say about people as being his children?

God the Father

The Bible often refers to God as a Father, one of the three persons of the Trinity (Father, Son and Holy Spirit). This holds true in both the Old and New Testaments, though Jesus' teachings make it more evident. The following passages depict God in the role of primary caregiver in the Old Testament:

- Deuteronomy 32:6: "Is this the way you repay the Lord, you foolish and unwise people? Is he not your Father, your Creator, who made you and formed you?"

- Jeremiah 31:33: Through the prophet, God says, "'I will be their God, and they will be my people'."

- Isaiah 63:16-17: "You are our Father, though Abraham does not know us and Israel does not acknowledge us; you, O Lord, are our Father, our Redeemer from old is your name."

- Isaiah 64:8: "O Lord, you are our Father; we are the clay and you are our potter; we are all the work of your hand."

- Isaiah 49:15-16: "'Can a mother forget the baby at her breast and have no compassion on the child she has borne? Though she may forget, I will not forget you! See, I have engraved you on the palms of my hands; your walls are ever before me.'"

- Psalm 103:13: "As a father has compassion on his children, so the Lord has compassion on those who fear him."

Then, in the New Testament, Jesus calls God Father and encourages us to do the same: When Jesus' disciples ask him to teach them how to pray, he tells them to start their prayers with: "Our Father, who art in heaven" (Matthew 6:9). The Aramaic word used here,

'Abba Father,' conveys a term of affection that embodies an intimate personal relationship rooted in confidence and trust. Children commonly refer to Abba when speaking to their earthly fathers. Jesus employs the term to emphasise the special meaning of our relationship with God the Father. The Apostle Paul also adopts this term in Galatians 1:15-16 and Romans 8:15.

Children of God

Scripture also references God's people as being his children, often within the context of their relationship to God the Father:

- 1 John 3:1, "See what great love the Father has lavished on us, that we should be called children of God! And that is what we are!"

- 1 John 5:19, "We know that we are children of God..."

- Galatians 3:26, "So in Jesus Christ, you are all children of God through faith."

- John 1:12, "Yet to all who did receive him, to those who believed in his name, he gave the right to become children of God."

These references, taken together, clearly speak to a father-child relationship similar to the relationship between a caregiver and their child. The Old Testament depicts God as a father to the people of Israel. In the New Testament, he becomes the father of all who have come to him through faith in his Son, Jesus Christ. This consistent portrayal of God as a nurturing father suggests that the lessons we learned about attachment and caregiving can also apply to our relationship with God. Our different attachment styles (secure, avoidant, anxious, and disorganised) influence how we connect with God. These dynamics shape our spiritual lives.

The Circle of Security and the Bible

We previously referenced the Circle of Security as a picture of secure attachment, within which healthy early bonds form between a caregiver and their child. As we return to the Circle of Security, we will quickly see how the language of the Circle contains fundamentally biblical references, related to our connection to God. The same language applies equally to both of these relationships.

The circle we pictured earlier went out on one side from the secure base, representing the child going out and exploring. The circle returned on the other side to the safe haven, representing the child returning to the caregiver for reassurance and comfort. In Psalm 121:8, David says, "The Lord will watch over your coming and your going both now and forevermore." This portrays the same imagery and language as the circle and refers to "watch over me," one of the children's psychological needs when they go out exploring the world.

We find this idea of God watching over us in several places in scripture. In Psalm 32:8, we read: "I will instruct you and teach you in the way you should go; I will counsel you with my loving eye on you." In Genesis 16:13, Hagar describes God as El Roi, translated as the one who sees me. David uses a very similar Hebrew word in Psalm 23:1, where he says, "The Lord is my Shepherd." The shepherd watches over the sheep, as the one who sees them. Jesus picks up on this when he describes himself as the "good shepherd" in John 10:11.

The circle sets out other psychological needs, including "delight in me", "help me", "enjoy with me", "protect me", "comfort me" and "help me to organise my feelings":

- Psalm 41:11 (ESV): "By this I know that you delight in me…"

- Psalm 38:22, "Come quickly to help me, my Lord and my Saviour."

- Psalm 25:20, "Guard my life and rescue me; do not let me be put to shame, for I take refuge in you."

- Psalm 16:1, "Keep me safe, my God, for in you I take refuge."

- Psalm 94:19, "When anxiety was great within me, your consolation brought me joy."

- Psalm 71:21, "You will increase my honour and comfort me once more."

- Psalm 139:7, "Where can I go from your Spirit? Where can I flee from your presence?"

- Psalm 22:1 (quoted by Jesus upon the cross), "My God, My God, why have you forsaken me?"

These are just a few examples of verses from the Psalms that describe how God meets the psychological needs of his children as they come and go. God promises to meet our psychological needs whilst he watches over our going out and our coming in. He represents both our secure base from which we can confidently go out into the world and our safe haven to which we return when we are troubled. He remains "our refuge and strength, an ever-present help in trouble." (Psalm 46:1). This same language describes those early reciprocal bonds: God is our secure base, our safe haven, the one who stays close to us, and the one from whom we should fear being apart.

Psalm 23 - A Psalm of attachment

One psalm, in particular, could be fundamentally described as a psalm of attachment, which sums up these considerations in a beautifully poetic way. Psalm 23 says this:

> The Lord is my shepherd, I lack nothing.
> He makes me lie down in green pastures,
> he leads me beside quiet waters,
> he refreshes my soul.
> He guides me along the right paths
> for his name's sake.
> Even though I walk
> through the darkest valley,
> I will fear no evil,
> for you are with me;
> your rod and your staff,
> they comfort me.

You prepare a table before me
in the presence of my enemies.
You anoint my head with oil;
my cup overflows.
Surely your goodness and love will follow me
all the days of my life,
and I will dwell in the house of the Lord
forever.

Pause for thought

Take time to meditate on these few verses. Consider them within the context of everything we have explored about forging healthy bonds and reciprocal connection. Something about this psalm promotes a sense of well-being, peace, comfort and security, both now and in the future.

- How does it make you feel, reflecting on this psalm with a focus on your connection with God?

- Do these verses reflect your experience of your relationship with God?

- Or are there moments where you find yourself questioning, where your head says one thing, but your heart feels another? You are allowed to ask yourself those questions. These moments can lead to deeper understanding and connection.

Attachment styles and connection to the Father

This psalm describes what our relationship with God should and can look like. Unfortunately, it doesn't always line up with the original design. We learnt what early bonds and reciprocal connection look like from our earthly caregivers. They likely left a lasting impression which may or may not assist us in how well we connect to God. Our attachment style, which we explored in previous chapters, plays a part in how we connect with God as our father. Deborah Grey, who wrote *Attaching in Adoption*, says:

> I have come to acknowledge myself as an attachment-disordered child of a loving God. I am slow to trust and confused between life and God, in spite of evidence of love. I am grateful for this extravagant love, flowing through my life, through my work[1].

If you are secure in your attachment style, you often find trusting in God's care, provision and love easier and more natural. You can confidently explore the world using God as a secure base and know how faith is spelt R-I-S-K. You follow God's leading and divine guidance and return for comfort and reassurance when needed. You take great comfort in passages like Psalm 23, which resonate deeply with you, affirming the Lord as your shepherd and strong tower where you can take refuge. What the Bible tells you lines up with your experience, making it easier to believe these truths for yourself. But what happens when your experience of life and relationships differs from what you are being told by the Bible and in church?

---

1. Deborah Grey, *Attaching in Adoption* (Jessica Kinsley Publishers, 2012) p.9.

Here's where things get complicated. Our life experiences profoundly shape us, our beliefs and what we expect from ourselves and others. This distinction highlights the difference between what's often called 'head knowledge' and 'heart knowledge.' We might understand and agree with something in our minds, but it doesn't connect at a deeper level because of the impact of personal experiences linked to our attachment styles. If you are insecure in your attachment style, you may struggle to connect with God in several ways.

- <u>Avoidant attachment style</u>: If you have an avoidant attachment style, you might keep emotionally distant from God, relying more on your own understanding and strength. You may engage in religious disciplines out of a sense of duty rather than emotional connection. Routines like reading the Bible, praying and studying can make you feel connected to God without being too emotional. You might prefer to do things independently and find it hard to rely on God for help. Fully trusting God can be challenging because you might have learned not to trust others. You may struggle to experience a deep, personal relationship with God, seeing him more as a distant authority figure than a loving caregiver. You might avoid spiritual practices which require emotional vulnerability, keeping your spiritual life private and controlled. You may convince yourself you don't need close relationships with God or others to avoid feeling inadequate. Ironically, this can reinforce your feelings of inadequacy because you distance yourself from the very source of love and acceptance.

- <u>Anxious attachment style</u>: If you have an anxious attachment style, you might feel insecure in your relationship with God and constantly seek his validation and reassurance. You may often worry about your salvation and fear losing your faith or that God will abandon you, especially if you feel you are not living up to spiritual expectations. You might need frequent signs of God's presence to feel emotionally stable and become upset when you don't sense him near. Your view of God may fluctuate based on your emotional state. During hard times, God may feel distant and unresponsive, leading to more spiritual anxiety. You may also compare yourself to others, feeling you continually fall spiritually short. You may see others as closer to God or more worthy of his love, which can give rise to feelings of jealousy and self-doubt. The fear you are not good enough can cause you to feel as though you are on the sidelines, believing that God's promises of redemption and closeness are for everyone except you. You try very hard to stay close to God, thinking it depends on your efforts and you must prove your worthiness. This can lead to a strict following of religious rules (legalism) to feel you must do enough to earn God's grace, giving you a sense of control and reducing your anxiety about your relationship with him.

- <u>Disorganised attachment style</u>: If you have a disorganised attachment style, you might feel torn between wanting closeness to God and fearing his rejection. This may result in a chaotic spiritual life, with times of intense devotion and times of spiritual withdrawal. You might struggle with feelings of shame and think of yourself as unlovable and unwanted, which affects how you relate to God. You might be very hard on yourself, believing you deserve it and hoping God will be kinder to you if you punish yourself enough. You want closeness to God but fear judgement and rejection. Instead of feeling God delights in you, you might feel the opposite. You may think you need to achieve perfection to be acceptable to God, leading you to focus on strict religious practices to try to earn his approval. You may believe you fit in a special category of people who cannot experience God's love and redemption, whilst others can. Healing from this attachment style involves developing a consistent and trusting relationship with God, often with the help of a supportive faith community and therapeutic interventions to address past trauma.

Our attachment style can significantly impact our relationship with God, particularly how we feel we should relate to him. A secure attachment leads to a personal, intimate, healthy relationship with God. Deep connection recognises grace as the foundation of this relationship, placing less emphasis on our efforts to connect with him.

In contrast, for various reasons, an insecure attachment makes us feel like we have to take matters into our own hands, believing that the depth of the relationship depends on our efforts. If we internalised conditions of worth in childhood (as discussed in Chapter 2), we may feel we must meet these conditions to gain God's acceptance, value and love. If not met, they can make us feel unworthy of God. Whether driven by a need for comfort and safety, fear, or shame, the result remains the same: the emphasis on grace diminishes.

As we have looked more into the practical implications of the different attachment styles, you may have started to get a clearer picture of your attachment style. As you think about your connection to God, maybe you recognise some of these characteristics in you. Understanding your attachment style helps you to work out how you might better connect to the Father and, therefore, constitutes an essential part of your healing journey. Understanding the connection between attachment styles and approaches to spirituality can be incredibly valuable in pastoral care and personal spiritual growth. By recognising these tendencies, you can move towards a healthy, grace-based relationship with God avoiding the pitfalls of trying to do it all in your own strength and fostering true intimacy with God.

It is very good to be me

When considering what hinders the formation of healthy bonds and reciprocal connection, we noted that the process involves a two-way street. I mentioned it took no more than thirty-five seconds to accept Christ into my life, yet accepting me took the best part of the next thirty-five years. Like many who did not grow up with a secure attachment style, I struggled with issues around self-esteem and self-image and was not particularly optimistic about life.

Without a developed sense of self and an understanding of identity, I struggled with boundaries, autonomy and healthy relationships. Since I did not feel good about myself, this impacted my relationships with others. I projected onto them how I felt about myself.

We do the same with God. We think he feels and thinks about us, the way we feel and think about ourselves. Therefore, we must allow God to change our thoughts and feelings about ourselves. Part of the journey towards healing through connection to the Father requires us coming to terms with this truth: It is very good to be me. I can assure you this holds fundamentally true for everyone, including you. I have not always been assured of this in my life, but I do now to a much greater degree. You, too, can know deep down how very good it is to be you.

Connecting with a loving heavenly father offers a profound and life-changing experience. This connection forms the cornerstone of our spiritual journey, grounding us with a secure base and safe haven—both essential to attachment. Through this divine relationship, we begin to understand the true nature of God's unconditional love.

However, understanding and connecting with God's love represents only part of the journey. To fully embrace this relationship and experience the depth of healing and transformation it offers, we must also learn to see ourselves as God sees us. This shift in perspective directly impacts how we relate to God, ourselves and others. Seeing ourselves through God's eyes (valued, loved and cherished) can transform our self-esteem, heal our deepest wounds and empower us to live out our true identity as his beloved children.

Prayer

Where can I go from your Spirit?
Where can I flee from your presence?
If I go up to the heavens, you are there;
if I make my bed in the depths, you are there.
If I rise on the wings of the dawn,
if I settle on the far side of the sea,
even there your hand will guide me,
your right hand will hold me fast.
Psalm 139:7-10

Heavenly Father, we thank you for your loving care and compassion towards us. We thank you for your promise you would never leave us or forsake us and we can go nowhere to hide from you. Open our hearts to experience your nurturing presence in every moment of our lives. Help us to lean into your care, knowing you hold us close and guide us with tenderness and wisdom.

In Jesus' name. Amen.

Chapter 6

Seeing Yourself as the Father Sees You

We can have a profound connection with a loving heavenly Father, viewing him as our primary caregiver. The other side to this divine relationship involves understanding how the Father sees us. Knowing how God perceives and values us helps us to embrace our identity as his beloved children. Seeing ourselves through his eyes can heal from past wounds and deepen our sense of worth and belonging.

Fearfully and wonderfully made

Does God make mistakes? Your initial reaction likely comes as an emphatic "No!" He would not be God if he could make mistakes, and certainly not God in any way we would recognise. But have you ever wondered if he did make a mistake when he created you? This reflects less on him than on how you feel about yourself.

In Genesis 1:31, on the sixth day, after he had created mankind in his own image, we read, "God saw all that he had made, and it was very good." When God made man, he saw how it was very good. It is, therefore, very good to be me and very good to be you. When you look in the mirror, I wonder whether you ever look at yourself and think: Yes, I agree, 'it is very good to be me'.

Psalm 139:13-14 says: "For you created my inmost being; you knit me together in my mother's womb. I praise you because I am fearfully and wonderfully made; your works are wonderful; I know that full well." King David asserts he is fearfully and wonderfully made. The same truth applies to you and I. Do you know deep down how wonderfully and fearfully God created you? A lot of the time, we do mental gymnastics to try to get around this stuff. This verse does not apply to us since we are in a special category, meaning we are somehow different and excluded.

The dangers of comparing ourselves to others

Then, we complicate matters by comparing ourselves to others. We look at successful people and assume they have unique qualities we don't have. We put them in a particular category to justify how we think about ourselves because we don't have those qualities or talents. We all tend to doubt ourselves and suffer from impostor syndrome. Impostor syndrome causes a person to doubt their abilities and fear people might find out they are a fraud.

Most people have struggled with this at some point or even consistently. Many very successful people deep down see themselves as inadequate and mediocre despite evidence of their high levels of skill, accomplishment and talent. In an interview with Vogue in 2013, Emma Watson, who played Hermione in the Harry Potter films, said:

> Now when I receive recognition for my acting, I feel incredibly uncomfortable. I tend to turn in on myself. I feel like an imposter… Any moment, someone's going to find out I'm a total fraud, and that I don't deserve any of what I've achieved.

The challenge with comparison lies in the need to compare like for like. What the so-called special person excels at is simply being themselves. You are the only person uniquely qualified to be you. No one else can take your place and no one could ever do a better job of it. God created you to be you, not anyone else. When God made you, he saw that you were very good. Realising this truth can be quite a journey—I've certainly wrestled with it myself.

A personal journey of self-discovery

I preached a sermon *It is Very Good to be Me* at Grace Church Wolverhampton (my home church) in March 2022. This was only two days after we had decided the charity I had spent eight years building would have to enter into liquidation. At the time, I still felt it was very good to be me despite my circumstances. Just because I was going through a hard time and facing some significant personal challenges, my identity was not impacted, and the truth was still the truth. The process wasn't easy, but it was powerful and liberating. A central theme of this sermon was my testimony, a journey of discovery of both God's identity and mine.

The journey of self-discovery began when I first listened to the podcast *Intentional Family*. Jon Tyson was talking specifically about the "involved father". This father objectively does it all right and gets involved, but there may be something missing in the relationship regarding personal connection. The "involved father" does not quite get you for who you are. As I realised this was how I felt, God started showing me how my dad never stood a chance. God spoke to me about how and who he created me to be. He said something like this: "Matt, I created you to be weird by most people's standards, but not in a bad way." 'Weird' is just 'wired' spelt differently. God had wired me differently. This holds true of everyone. But those who know me know I have a very different way of thinking than most people.

As I thought about this, I realised my parents, my brother and my classmates never stood a chance because of the way God had wired me. And since I was beginning to see it was very good to be me, being wired differently was ok. I realised I had probably held offence in my heart for many years, feeling like my parents, at the very least, should be able to get me. So, I had an open, honest conversation with them about this. They had found it difficult, as had others, too.

Through our conversation, I could let go of the offence I had been carrying and found much more peace. I had a similar discussion with my wife, who pointed out how in almost every argument we have ever had, I probably shouted something like: "You just don't get it do you?" And of course, she didn't, and I had to realise this was OK too. Not long after those conversations, on my way to the hairdresser, a thought popped into my head: *"You've always felt as though no one gets you, and everybody is out to get you; isn't it a wonder you've struggled your whole life with a spirit of frustration and anger."* I was immediately set free from the power of those thoughts. That way of thinking had been identified as a lie. A new way of thinking was beginning to replace it.

Roadblocks on the pathways in our minds

Our minds often develop stubborn ways of thinking that we might not consciously consider, much like pathways we've walked so frequently they seem like the only routes available. These mental pathways can stem from painful experiences in our childhood or hurtful words spoken over us by others which we have accepted as true. They become part of shaping our beliefs and expectations of ourselves and others. We learned earlier how our early bonds and reciprocal connections can have similar impacts. Over time, these routes become so familiar we accept them as truths about ourselves and the world.

Imagine these pathways in our minds. Sometimes, they lead us to roadblocks—negative beliefs about our worth or the intentions of others. In front of these roadblocks, we see diversion signs pointing us to a new path that works its way around the obstacle. These roadblocks aren't just harmless barriers. Behind them, you may find negative influences thriving on our fears and falsehoods. For me, there was a roadblock in my mind with a diversion sign linked to the thought that everyone was out to get me, and no one got me. So, my brain created a new pathway which went around the obstacle. However, this new pathway did not lead to the same destination as the old pathway. Behind the roadblock was a pathway waiting to be built in my mind that would have led to autonomy, healthy boundaries and healthy relationships. Instead, I went off on a diversion for years that impacted my self-esteem, relationships with others and God.

Toxic thinking

I am painfully aware of stories of others who have encountered such roadblocks in their thinking that have similarly impacted them. Through self-reflection and counselling, a close friend of mine realised how for years, they had held on to what they call a toxic thought: "I don't matter. No one would notice if I was gone, and they would be better off without me."

Contemplating the havoc such a thought could wreak on your mind proves difficult. Surely, this cannot be true. Yet my friend believed it, and that's what matters. You may have a similar stubborn way of thinking about yourself, so embedded in your mind that it would be hard even to imagine calling it into question. You might not even realise. There are a few things you can do to explore this for yourself:

- Take some time to reflect and think about the stories you tell yourself about yourself. What negative things do you find yourself saying?

- Daily journaling might help you identify patterns of thinking and how they could be affecting your behaviour and emotions.

- Pray and ask the Holy Spirit to guide you in this process of self-discovery. Proverbs 3:6 says: "In all your ways submit to him, and he will make your paths straight." God promises that when we submit to him and seek his will for our lives, he will guide us and direct us on straight paths. This brings us back to when we spoke about pathways in the brain where roadblocks stand in the way and our brains find a way to go around the obstacle. God promises to make those paths straight again.

- Ask trusted wise friends if they can help guide you as well.

- Seek professional help as needed. Cognitive behavioural therapy (CBT) can make a significant difference in reframing your thinking and dealing with toxic thoughts.

- Once you have identified a toxic thought, challenge it. Determine if any evidence to the contrary exists.

- Then, find something true about you which can replace the lie and toxic thinking. This could be a bible verse or a memory opposed to the toxic thought. Write it on a Post-it note and put it somewhere prominent so you see it often.

- If you feel comfortable, share this process with someone else. Hold yourself accountable for what you believe and think about yourself with someone you trust. Ask them to help you by reminding you of who you are.

Pause for thought

I recommend you check out another video (from Sprouts) at this point which might help enhance your understanding, using a real-life example. Head over to YouTube and search for Sprouts, *Cognitive Behavioural Therapy (CBT)*. This great resource highlights some practical steps towards transformation through the renewing of your mind.

We have just thought about some tools and how they might help you to identify toxic thoughts negatively impacting your life. Take some time to consider how you might use them. Some simple questions may assist you in identifying toxic thoughts:

1. What am I thinking and feeling right now?

2. Is this thought based on facts or assumptions?

3. Do I exaggerate or expect the worst possible outcome?

4. What do I know or have I experienced that might challenge the validity of this thought?

5. How does this thought impact my mood and my behaviour?

6. Could I view things in a kinder way leading to more constructive outcomes?

Knowing God and being known by him

I didn't know much about this kind of process at the time, but God, in his gracious sovereignty, decided to lead me through it. He impressed upon me a new truth: he understands me profoundly and remains always there for me. God exposed the lie. He removed the roadblock. The negative influences hiding behind the roadblock lost their grip. Understanding I am known and loved by my creator replaced the lie that had isolated me. This truth freed me from the negative patterns, showing me how God, who created me, truly gets me. Now the roadblock had been removed, I was free to build this new pathway, which would lead me to a place of more optimism, feeling better connected and more positive about myself. It is after all very good to be me. The impact on my life and my relationships has been transformational. What more do we need in this life than to know God and be known by him?

In the Old Testament, King David talks about this: In 1 Samuel 7:20, he says, "For you know your servant, O Sovereign Lord." In Psalm 139:23-24, he speaks of his desire to be known by God when he says: "Search me, God, and know my heart; test me and know my anxious thoughts. See if there is any offensive way in me and lead me in the way everlasting." In the New Testament, in Galatians 4:7-8, Paul says: "Formerly, when you did not know God, you were slaves to those who by nature are not gods. But now that you know God—or rather are known by God—how is it that you are turning back to those weak and miserable forces?" For Paul, knowing God and being known by God liberates us and leads us to a greater measure of personal freedom. In other words, healing comes through connection to the Father.

God knows everything about me. "Nothing in all creation is hidden from God's sight. Everything is uncovered and laid bare before the eyes of him to whom we must give an account" (Hebrews 4:13). The NLT renders this as: "All are naked and exposed before him."

He knows everything about us, including the wrong things we have done in the past and the wrong things we will do in the future. And yet still he sent his son to die so we might be forgiven and might enter into the freedom of knowing him and being known by him.

This speaks directly to the shame experienced by those with insecure attachment styles, particularly the disorganised type. God already knows everything about you and still desires a relationship. In John 10:15, Jesus says: 'I am the good shepherd; I know my sheep, and my sheep know me—just as the Father knows me and I know the Father—and I lay down my life for the sheep.' Despite knowing all there is to know about you, God still sent his only Son, Jesus, to die for you. Understanding this truth leads to one conclusion: it is very good to be you.

God made you in his image. He uniquely gifted you. He has a plan for your life (Jeremiah 29:11). He has placed you within a church family and has given you a part to play in the family: "From him, the whole body joined and held together by every supporting ligament, grows and builds itself up in love, as each part does its work." (Ephesians 4:16). He has prepared good works in advance for you to do (Ephesians 2:10). God invites you today to step into his story and embrace your role. In Revelation 21:5, we read: "He who was seated on the throne said: 'I am making everything new'." This represents the greater plan and bigger picture.

Stepping into his story

His story unfolds around the restoration and redemption of all things. And he wants your involvement. He wants to use you to further his purposes to make all things new. How do you do that? First and foremost, by being you. He designed and created you with a purpose in mind. He made you to be you, gifted you and prepared good works for you to do. By discovering who you are and the potential he has placed within you, you can put your potential, skills and talents to work, bringing glory to him and enabling others to thrive. You can be part of his story.

Yet you won't ever take that step if you do not accept yourself for who he has made you to be. You have to overcome impostor syndrome and the fear of being found out as a fraud. I used to think I should be disqualified just for being me because I was weird. God showed me how the opposite holds true. I am qualified because he made me who I am, not by accident but by design. And my weirdness does not disqualify me but actually qualifies me in his eyes.

Fulfilling his plans for me and stepping into his story requires confidence, but not confidence in me. I can have confidence in who he created me to be, confidence in the gifts he has placed in me and confidence in the fact that his blood covers my sins. Whatever comes next, he has got this. If I am truly confident in him, then I can be assured he has created, purposed and planned very good things and it is very good to be me.

Sometimes, we have to revisit these things, just like when we talked about peeling off the layers of an onion. We asked if God can make mistakes. In early 2023, I was out on a late-night walk with a very close friend of mine (Chris) and his dog (Snoopy). At one point, I found myself lamenting out loud:

> God I do not believe you are who you say you are. You cannot be God and make mistakes. Yet you have made a mistake. I am the least patient, most angry, frustrated and difficult person I know. Yet you have given me a wife with significant struggles with past wounds. You have given me two adopted children with special needs and attachment issues. We cannot make this work. I cannot do this. You have got this wrong and therefore you cannot be God!

This may have been the single most honest conversation I had ever had with God. My words seemed somewhat disrespectful, but I do believe God wants us to be honest with him. We may struggle with a number of issues when we bring our insecure attachment styles to our relationship with God: emotional distance, not seeking help, trying to do it in your own strength and feeling ashamed and inadequate (in a wrong way). This conversation was me opening myself up to God, inviting him into my raw pain. I was admitting I was not perfect and needed his help. All of this showed awkwardly how as I became more comfortable being me, I was beginning to exhibit earned secure attachment traits in how I related to my heavenly father. A healing process had begun through connection to God the Father.

We can relate to the Father in a way that promotes reciprocal connection and healing. We can learn more about this through considering what this looked like for some of the characters from the Bible. Valuable insight comes, for example, from considering the impact of Joseph's secure attachment to Jacob or the insecure attachment styles of King David, King Saul and Samson. The example of their lives helps us better understand how this relates to us personally.

Prayer

> Isaiah 43:1: "But now, this is what the Lord says—he who created you, Jacob, he who formed you, Israel: 'Do not fear, for I have redeemed you; I have summoned you by name; you are mine.'"

Heavenly Father, we thank you we can have confidence in who you created us to be. Open our eyes to see ourselves the way you see us. Bring us a revelation of who we are in you so we may connect with you in a deeper and more meaningful way. May your Holy Spirit help us to see where we may be thinking untrue thoughts and lead us in bringing your light into dark places in our minds. Open our eyes to see ourselves the way you see us. Bring us a revelation of who we are in you so we may connect with you in a deeper and more meaningful way.

In Jesus' name. Amen.

Chapter 7

Examples and Warnings from the Word

We are seeking to see ourselves as the Father sees us. This perspective can profoundly impact our identity and sense of worth. Now, let's turn our attention to the Bible for practical examples and warnings. Through the stories of various biblical characters, we'll uncover lessons on relationships and the consequences of our choices. By examining these scriptural narratives, we can gain valuable insights and guidance for our own journey towards deeper connection and spiritual growth. "These things happened to them as examples and were written down as warnings for us, on whom the culmination of the ages has come." (1 Cor:10-11)

Paul tells us that biblical accounts were recorded so we can learn from their experiences. There are some great examples in the Bible of people who show traits of different attachment styles: secure, anxious, avoidant and disorganised. We briefly mentioned characters like Joseph, Jonah, Saul and Samson, and we will further develop those thoughts. Again, I do not seek to provide an in-depth psychoanalysis or diagnose anyone. However, by observing the characteristics and traits of attachment styles in their lives, we can see how psychology and theology might complement each other more than we previously thought. There may also be some warnings for us to heed and examples from which we can learn.

Joseph exhibits traits of secure attachment

Consider Joseph, for example. He was Jacob's favourite. Genesis 37:3 says, "Jacob loved Joseph more than he did any of his other sons because Joseph was born when Jacob was very old." Joseph had a great relationship with his earthly father. Therefore, we should expect Joseph to grow up feeling connected, optimistic and having a positive self-image. He should be able to handle stress, communicate openly, manage conflict well and respond well to other people's needs.

Joseph unwisely shares his dreams of his brothers bowing to him, leading to their betrayal. They sell him into slavery and tell their father how Joseph died. Can you just imagine the shock and heartbreak Joseph must have felt when his own brothers-those he trusted and grew up with – turned on him so violently. He wasn't betrayed by strangers but by his own family who threw him into a pit, sold him like property and ripped him away from everything he knew. The ones who were supposed to protect him, became the very people who sent him away. A betrayal like this could easily have caused him to harden his heart, leaving him closed off and distrustful for the rest of his life. And yet, Joseph's story doesn't go that way.

Despite this early betrayal, Joseph continually builds trusting relationships. He gains favour with Potiphar, who puts him in charge of his household. However, he ends up in prison as a result of a false allegation of rape. In prison, Joseph earns the trust of the warden, who puts him in charge of the prisoners. After being released, the cupbearer also betrays him when he forgets to mention him to Pharoah. Each of these betrayals—the injustice of Potiphar's wife's false accusation, the cupbearer's broken promise, the years of being forgotten in prison—could have been the final straw. Most of us would have withdrawn, built walls and given up on trusting anyone. But Joseph's ability to trust again, to build new relationships despite his past, reflects not just resilience but a deep, secure sense of his own worth and purpose. His trust wasn't naive; it was grounded in a confidence that his story wasn't over, that even in the darkest moments, God was still at work.

Jospeh interprets Pharaoh's dreams and gains his trust. Pharoah appoints him to manage the country. He demonstrates his ability to form strong relationships despite repeated betrayals. Joseph's trust in others and his resilience reflect his confidence in his own worth and his ability to adapt and thrive in adverse situations. When reunited with his brothers, he shows empathy, compassion and forgiveness, recognising God's role in his journey. This response highlights his emotional stability and secure attachment. In Genesis 50:20, he says, "You intended to harm me, but God intended it for good to accomplish what is now being done, the saving of many lives." Joseph's strong relationship with his father, Jacob, likely played a crucial role in his resilience and ability to maintain trust and stability throughout his life. This early secure attachment enabled him to persevere and succeed despite numerous challenges. Joseph's journey showcases traits of a secure attachment style, marked by his ability to form healthy relationships, maintain emotional stability and trust in God's plan.

> **Pause for thought**
>
> Think about how you might feel, when everything seems to be going wrong, not knowing what would happen next. If you are not confident in the outwork of God's plan for your life, you might, like me, be tempted to think that everything and everyone seeks to conspire against you. I have often felt such emotions, focussing on how life continued to beat me whilst I was down.
>
> - Have you been in a similar situation?
>
> - How did you feel?
>
> - How easy do you find it to trust God's plan for your good, even when circumstances suggest otherwise?

Resisting sexual temptation

We can learn much from Joseph's story in the area of resisting sexual temptation. He found himself in a compromising situation where Potiphar's wife was literally throwing herself at him. He resisted the temptation and fled from her advances. Joseph had a strong sense of identity and a strong moral compass in line with his secure attachment. Resisting temptation isn't necessarily primarily about how well he resists sin. Knowing his identity and self-worth helps him to overcome. Joseph says, "How then could I do such a wicked thing and sin against God?" (Genesis 39:9). He knows how giving in to his master's wife would not align with his character, the respect he has for his master and his personal integrity. He holds himself accountable to God and himself in a remarkable way.

Many Christians struggle in this area of sexual temptation, and it could be linked to an insecure attachment style. Struggles with pornography, for example, may not be solely physical: they may be seeking emotional comfort and fulfilling unmet needs for intimacy and validation (anxious attachment style), or they may be avoiding emotional closeness whilst maintaining a sense of control and distance in relationships (avoidant attachment style); Or amidst the turmoil of their emotions and chaotic life, they may be seeking a means of escape or self-medicating to deal with stress, anxiety or depression (disorganised attachment style).

The pathway to freedom may begin with recognising that the behaviour could be rooted in a struggle with underlying negative emotions and unfulfilled needs. This more compassionate understanding might help an individual explore other ways to fulfil those needs or deal with those emotions in a healthier context.

A friend of mine, who will remain anonymous, struggled for many years with an addiction to pornography. A great deal of shame accompanied this. Independently of this, they were also exploring issues around their insecurities, mainly connected to their early relationships and some toxic thinking. As they moved from a previously insecure attachment style towards traits of earned secure attachment, it got easier to resist temptation and overcome. Interestingly, the link between the two only ever became clear with hindsight rather than being something they had set out to achieve. They are now able to look back and see how their feelings and unmet needs have been a big part of their addiction.

Identity at the heart of walking in freedom

Freedom in Christ offers a course designed to help Christians experience the freedom Jesus Christ won for them. The course's language aligns well with concepts from attachment theory. The writers suggest we lost our sense of "security, significance and acceptance" through the Fall. Jesus restores these things to us. The course guides participants through personal reflection, ministry and building new relationships based on intimacy and trust. The content addresses themes of identity, self-worth, emotional regulation and relationship building. The course encourages participants to move towards earned secure attachment, even though it doesn't explicitly use attachment terminology. Participating in a Freedom in Christ course could benefit personal and spiritual growth.

The Freedom in Christ course starts by exploring identity. If you see yourself as a redeemed sinner, you find your identity in being a sinner. And what do sinners do? They sin. To resist the temptation to sin, you must first realise you are a saint who occasionally sins. Since your identity is that of a saint, sin no longer forms part of your identity. You may still slip up and occasionally fall back into your old ways, but it no longer defines who you are. Joseph had a strong sense of his identity. He knew who he was. A strong sense of identity as a child of God the Father forms the foundation for living a life of righteousness and holiness. Identity empowers us to overcome sin.

Pause for thought

This way of thinking may be new to you. You may not have realised before that sin relates as much to who you are or who you believe yourself to be as to what you do.

- How does this make you feel?
- Have you ever thought about this link between sin and identity?
- Do you see yourself as a redeemed sinner or as a saint, a child of the most High God?

A child who truly respects, loves and admires their dad wants to be just like them. The same holds true in our relationship with God. The more connected we are to the Father, the more we will find our identity in his son, Jesus Christ, and the more he will empower us to walk in freedom.

King David's secure attachment to God

King David offers another fascinating biblical character, though less straightforward than Joseph. The Psalms, many of which David wrote, including Psalm 23, are full of references to traits of secure attachment to God. He sees God as his secure base and safe haven. He keeps close to God and exhibits signs of distress when he feels separation from him. David developed a close relationship with God while looking after the sheep in the fields. He learned to trust God. He learned to express his emotions openly and with vulnerability. This carries over into his compassionate and caring leadership style. This demonstrates secure attachment style. He appears secure in his relationship with God.

Contrary to Joseph, David gives in to sexual temptation when he commits adultery with Bathsheba. Even individuals with a generally secure attachment to God can fail badly due to human weakness and vulnerability to temptation. When Nathan, the prophet, confronts him, David repents genuinely and remorsefully (see Psalm 51). This cycle of sin, repentance and forgiveness reflects the dynamics of a secure relationship where he feels safe to return and seek reconciliation despite his failures. We can glean great hope from this aspect of King David's life story.

King David's experiences illustrate how a deeply flawed individual can still maintain a strong relationship with God. They can seek and receive forgiveness and ultimately fulfil their divine purpose despite numerous significant personal failings. This comes as good news if you struggle to recognise that it's very good to be you, despite some of the awful things you've done. Ultimately, scripture describes David, despite everything, as "a man after his (God's) own heart" (1 Samuel 13:14) because of the depth of relationship and connection they enjoyed together. You, too, can experience a similar depth of connection to God and be described as a man or woman after God's own heart.

King David's insecure attachment with his family

There is, however, more to King David and his story. In his relationship with his family, things are far less secure. David keeps emotional distance from his children and fails to exercise his parental responsibilities. In 1 Kings 1:6, we are told explicitly about his son Adonijah: "His father had never rebuked him by asking, "Why do you behave as you do?" Interestingly, the Bible comments about David's parenting and discipline of his children, suggesting this contributed towards the ongoing saga of family conflict and tensions.

This forms part of a pattern of behaviour. When his son Amnon rapes his sister, David fails to take action, which leads to Absalom taking matters into his own hands, murdering his brother and rebelling against the throne. David's parenting style remains hands-off and emotionally distant, lacking clear leadership and guidance. He further exacerbates the conflict between his children by showing favouritism towards Solomon causing further conflict and strife in his family. In relation to his family and his children in particular, David shows traits of an avoidant attachment style.

This should come as no surprise. David spent much time on his own, away from his family and brothers, tending to the sheep. When Samuel comes to their house to anoint a new king, David's dad only belatedly remembers he has another son tending to the sheep in the fields. His father seems to have completely forgotten his existence (1 Samuel 16:11).

His brothers also have a negative attitude towards him. In 1 Samuel 17, we read: "When Eliab, David's oldest brother, heard him speaking with the men, he burned with anger at him and asked, "Why have you come down here? And with whom did you leave those few sheep in the wilderness? I know how conceited you are and how wicked your heart is; you came down only to watch the battle."

He has nothing but contempt for David and speaks down on him. His other brothers may have been the same. Taking all of this into consideration, it seems fair that he should show traits of an avoidant attachment style, characterised by emotional withdrawal and a lack of guidance and discipline. Yet, he also moves towards a healthier, more connected and vital relationship with his creator.

Hope for change

The Bible shows us hope for change. The way things begin does not have to be the same as how they end. King David journeyed towards earned secure attachment to God, even though things with his family were all over the place. He found a measure of healing through connection to the Father in the fields with the sheep. You may not have had the best start, but things can change. You may not manage to turn around the relationships with your family because it does not depend on just you. You can, however, move towards earning a secure attachment to God and others. And maybe you can go one step further than David in stopping the generational pattern of insecure attachment in your family.

My friend Sam grew up with a narcissistic mother who was more concerned about meeting her own needs than she was his. He developed an anxious attachment style. He went through years of therapy, counselling and personal reflection. Yet, step by step, he grew into feeling more confident in himself, more assertive of his own needs and opinions and more secure in healthy relationships with good boundaries. The trigger for wanting to change came when he had children and realised he had to find a way to do things differently. He confronted his attachment insecurities and began to work on connecting with his children in ways his parents never did.

King Saul's attachment insecurities

Another character we referenced concerning insecure attachment was King Saul. We know very little about his upbringing; however, we may gain some insight from what we see of him later in life. King Saul was God's anointed and chosen King for Israel. The plan was for him to follow the Lord's commands and lead from his relationship with God. Unfortunately, Saul does not always do what the Lord tells him. In 1 Samuel 13, Samuel told him to wait for him for seven days to teach him patience and dependence on God. Saul failed the test. He got impatient and went ahead and sacrificed the burnt offering himself. In 1 Samuel 15, God commanded Saul to eradicate the Amalekites, yet he spared King Agag and brought back some sheep and cattle to offer as sacrifices. Saul's disobedience and lack of trust in God demonstrate traits of an anxious attachment style.

Saul was trying to stay close to God through his own efforts. His anxiety about the kingdom being taken away from him, led him to overcompensate and take matters into his own hands. In addition to this, his relationship with David gives us much insight. His jealousy of David's success, betrayed his underlying need for affirmation and validation. In 1 Samuel 18:7, the women praise the victories in battle, saying, "Saul has slain his thousands and David his ten thousands." This makes Saul angry. He perceives David to be a threat to the throne and the kingdom and so, on numerous occasions, attempts to kill. Yet, at other times, he speaks to him as to a son (e.g. 1 Samuel 24:16) and displays affection towards him. This emotional back and forth constitutes another trait of anxious attachment: He wants to be close to David and yet continually pushes him away.

Saul teaches us just how much God values obedience. This so often, however, requires trust, especially when things don't seem to be going according to plan, or we have to wait. If we are insecurely attached, we may be like Saul and take matters into our own hands. When we do so, we might hear ourselves saying to God, "I did it

for you." And God's response may be, "I wanted to do it **with** you. We could have done it together." As a relational God, he wants to connect with us. He doesn't behave like an adrenaline junkie who takes pleasure in making us wait until the last possible minute. His way is good, the best, with perfect timing. How we handle the waiting speaks more about our attachment style than about who God is and how He operates.

More hope for change

My wife Rachel had her fair share of struggles growing up and developed an anxious attachment style as a result. She has never really considered herself as a leader. Despite this, she agreed at the beginning of this academic year to become chair of the governing board of our local primary school. This has been such a steep learning curve. So often, when she went to meetings, she felt like she was a twelve-year-old again, fearful of the Headteacher. Many of her emotions were linked to her attachment insecurities. She spoke to a therapist to help her deal with some of this. Now, we are doing family therapy together. Our family therapist is helping us to make sense of our world, be ourselves and thrive whilst parenting children with attachment issues and additional needs.

Rachel's confidence in bringing the right balance of support and challenge to the school (as chair of governors) has grown massively. She has stepped into leading from a place of earned secure attachment. Compassion, consistency, dependability, resilience and adaptability, now all characterise her leadership. She has begun to build relationships of trust across the school and brings so much of her brilliance to the role. This was formally recognised by the governing body in a recent review of her role and input. She now shows more confidence in being herself and trusting how God qualifies the called rather than calling the qualified.

Samson's erratic relationships and self-destructive behaviour

Finally, we come to Samson. As he grows up, he seems to exhibit traits of a disorganised attachment style. His erratic behaviour, filled with mixed signals, confuses others. His relationships fluctuate with great highs and lows. He struggles with trust issues, fear of rejection and difficulties forming close connections. Samson keeps getting into bed with the wrong women. In Judges 14, he tells his parents of his desire to marry a Philistine woman. Despite his Nazarite vow and the promises spoken over his life, Samson did not trust God or depend on him. He says, "she is right in my eyes" (Judges 14:3). This expression is found throughout the book of Judges: "everyone did as they saw fit". His impulsive decision was a bad idea! Throughout, Samson acts recklessly and impulsively, showing no emotional restraint. His emotional reactions are very extreme when others have offended him, even slightly. He kills thirty people, and the woman he set out to marry, goes off with someone else.

His relationship with Delilah, another non-Jewish woman, brims with instability and conflict. She betrays him repeatedly, yet he stays with her and reveals the secret of his strength. The Philistines imprison him and gouge out his eyes. Samson had no clear long-term strategy and acted impulsively, leading to inconsistent actions. His tragic death aligns with this pattern of self-destructive behaviour. And yet, we read on several occasions how the Lord used him to take down the Philistines. In the end, he killed many more of them when he died than he did during his life. Again, we encounter another imperfect biblical character struggling with profound insecurity in their relationships. And yet, the sovereignty and hand of the Lord is with them in bringing about his purposes and plans. God uses our weaknesses, our imperfections and our insecurities. Therefore, there is hope we can be transformed and changed. God's plans can prevail even in our worst moments.

Pause for thought

Knowing how God uses flawed, insecure and often sinful characters in his story is reassuring. You may begin to see how your insecurities impact your life and relationships with God and others. These patterns are not random but identifiable and often carry over generations. Reflecting on these patterns now can be beneficial. Good patterns lead to positive outcomes across generations, while destructive patterns have adverse effects. We can always start changing our thoughts and feelings to establish good patterns. Considering the lives of biblical characters serves as both a warning and an invitation. There's a warning about the consequences of unaddressed issues and an invitation to "be transformed by the renewing of your mind" (Romans 12:2), offering hope for radical change.

- Do you notice patterns and trends of behaviour in your own life which could be generational?

- Might they be linked to your attachment style or some toxic thinking you may have started to identify?

- How do you feel reflecting on the origins of some of these patterns or trends?

- Do you realise they may not reflect your true personality? Making these connections may be liberating, bringing a sense of freedom and increasing your self-worth. You may wish to think this through.

We have already considered how to develop a better sense of self and deal with toxic thoughts. This is all part of a process through which we can experience healing through connection to the Father. The pathway to this healing is spiritual adoption into God's family. Through spiritual adoption, we connect to the Father through his son, Jesus Christ. God has made a way for us to be brought into right relationship with him. God cares for us perfectly within the context of our relationship with him. And since attachment is a two-way street, we will also dive into what we can do to help maintain the secure, loving, trust-filled connection from our perspective. Everything we have explored to this point sets the stage for our connection to a loving heavenly father. But how does this lead to healing? There are practical implications of our connection to God in bringing healing to our bodies, minds and souls. The pathway to healing comes through connection to the Father.

Prayer

"Your word is a lamp for my feet,
a light on my path." Psalm 119:105

Heavenly Father, as we explore both human and divine relationships in your Word, help us to see ourselves in these stories. Use these examples to teach us about your faithfulness and love. May we draw strength from the lessons and heed the warnings of the past and apply them to our relationships today. May your word enlighten our understanding of how we connect with you and thereby experience healing.

In Jesus' name. Amen.

Part III: Healing through connection to the Father

His Publishing Services Ltd

Chapter 8

The Healing Journey Begins with Spiritual Adoption

Sometimes the best interests of a child require removal from their birth family and placement within a new context. When things have gone horribly wrong, fostering and adoption provide a fresh start and a context within which a healing process can begin. The spiritual reality mirrors the natural one. Spiritual adoption commences the healing journey and provides the context within which we have a parent-child relationship with God the Father, which we covered in Part II.

Our early bonds affect our response to separation and distress from a young age. Using Mary Ainsworth's *Strange Situation* study, we examined how temporary separation from a mother causes a child to fear being apart from their carer. We can identify different attachment styles by observing how children react when reunited with their carer. These styles greatly influence their self-view and expectations of others. Those different attachment styles impact on how we connect to God as our father.

There are sadly, circumstances within which temporary separation ends up being permanent, and child services remove the child from the birth family and place them with a foster family or an adoptive family. More often than not, the child has already spent some time with their birth family. They may have experienced neglect, abuse or trauma. This can have a lasting impact on their development, certainly in the short term, but maybe in the long term, too.

Children are sometimes given up for adoption voluntarily, though this happens far less than it has in the past. They may only spend a short time in foster care before being adopted into their forever family. This may be sufficiently early for them to receive all the loving, nurturing care they need to build a healthy wall, which should have all the building blocks in place from a very early age. You would be forgiven for thinking they may not present with the same difficulties as children who have experienced neglect, abuse or trauma.

The Primal Wound

However, adoption can bring with it a deep sense of loss and abandonment for those given up at birth. Nancy Verrier, an adoptive mother and author, calls this deep emotional trauma the Primal Wound. This Primal Wound can create a longing for identity and a feeling of emptiness. These deep emotions can also confuse their identity and how they fit into their new family and the world. They may live in fear of rejection or abandonment. Since it has already happened once, what will stop it from happening again? These unresolved issues can impact the quality of the bonds they form with their caregivers (foster carers or adopters), leading to relational challenges and an insecure attachment style.

In the UK, social services advise adoptive families to be as open as possible about adoption from the earliest possible age. I personally favour this approach. This deep emotional trauma presents regardless since it results from the separation from the biological mother at an age critical to development. A bond has already formed between the birth mother and the baby in the womb. Both subconsciously early on and later consciously, breaking the bond has a profound impact. Children who only find out later on they are adopted often express how they had always felt or even known something was different.

The deep pain of the Primal Wound can be difficult to describe. Spanish poet Miguel Hernandez captures this feeling in his poem Elegia when he mourns the loss of a friend:

> The pain of you burrows into my side until it hurts simply to breathe. An icy blow, a sudden fist, a murderous swinging axe has laid you low and I weep for this disgrace and the thousand things that follow without end. This gaping wound won't be crossed and I feel your death more than I do this life.[1]

While the Primal Wound is often discussed in the context of adoption, this sense of loss, disconnection and longing for belonging isn't limited to adoptees. Many of us carry invisible wounds from relationships that were broken, emotional needs that went unmet, or life experiences that left us feeling abandoned or unseen. These wounds, whether tied to family, friendships, or other significant relationships, shape how we see ourselves and how we connect with others—and even with God. The need for identity, belonging and unconditional love is something we all share, no matter our life circumstances.

For adopted children, these feelings are often especially intense, as their journey often involves navigating both the loss of their birth family and the challenge of building new connections in their adoptive family. I asked a child I know who was adopted at birth how they felt about this. They found it understandably hard to put it in words. They expressed a lot of sadness at "going away" from

---

1. Translated from Spanish by Steve Kronen in a new manuscript entitled After Words – 50 Versions from Sappho to Claribel Alegría.

their birth family. Still, they felt a bit conflicted because it meant they ended up with their adoptive family, which was good. They said thinking about it made them "feel like they want to be held." They also expressed a sense of pain, "sometimes it hurts," and doubt as to whether the pain would ever go away. I am not sure I will ever completely understand, having not experienced what they have been through.

The Spiritual Primal Wound

Profound similarities exist between the impact of the Primal Wound and the experience of humanity following the Fall in Genesis 3. In the previous chapter, we considered this in terms of losing a sense of security, acceptance and significance. The Fall describes man's original disobedience and sin against God, which led to Adam and Eve being thrown out of the Garden of Eden. They were separated from God, and their disobedience led to the introduction of both physical and spiritual death. They also lost their innocence, direct connection to God and the harmony they had previously enjoyed. This loss has left mankind feeling an emptiness no worldly experiences could fill. People still try to fill the void with anything other than God, leading to all manner of forms of idolatry. For example, we worship and pursue other Gods rather than the one true God, our primary caregiver and source of love and genuine connection.

The separation from God could also be perceived as a form of abandonment by God. Although this did not happen, the perception can rival the reality in strength. This perception of abandonment has led to feelings of guilt, shame and rejection, which run deep in the soul. And it has also impacted what people think of God. Some of those who do not know him think of him as distant and emotionally unavailable. Others believe him to be harsh, angry and judgmental. Both the Primal Wound and the Fall lead to feelings of loss and abandonment, a search for identity and belonging, a fear of rejection and insecure attachment. The comparison strikes me enough to refer to the Fall as the Spiritual Primal Wound in humanity's soul. This has both individual and cosmic implications we feel deeply.

A longing for relational connection

Since I grew up thinking everyone was out to get me and no one got me, I felt as though I was missing something in terms of relational connection both to myself and to others, including God. Even after I became a Christian at a young age, there have still been times in my life when I have sought to fill the void I felt in me with anything other than God, including through things like sex, drugs and even joining a form of cult.

At university, I joined a fraternity which was probably not dissimilar to the frat houses we hear of or see on TV shows and films in America. We wore special berets and sang songs to the gods of alcohol and sex. Messing about seemed harmless enough at the time. Still, this was a not-so-subtle form of Idol worship, very similar to the practices of the Israelites in the Old Testament at the High Places.

I have already mentioned how much of my life has been a quest for identity and belonging, just wanting to find somewhere I could fit in and be liked. With hindsight, I believe my insecure attachment style led me to struggle to find what I was looking for in my relationship with God many years after I became a Christian. I had also internalised a "condition of worth". My sense of value, acceptance and love were linked to performance and achievement. At one point, I went so far as to express to my pastor how life might not be worth living if I wasn't more successful, in the way I perceived success at the time.

Pause for thought

You may be unable to relate strictly to my experience since it was a bit extreme. But you may be able to identify ways you have struggled to connect with God meaningfully, even after you became a Christian. Take a moment to reflect on whether any of this speaks to you.

- Are you still struggling with your sense of identity and belonging and trying to figure out how you fit in?

- Do you still experience feelings of loss or abandonment?

- Do you fear rejection because you are not good enough?

- Do you think and feel that your relationship with God has the depth it could have?

- Is God your secure base and safe haven, your ever-present help in times of trouble?

Even if you don't feel like you are there yet, I am hopeful that with some personal reflection, a loving community around you and a better understanding of these issues, you, too, like me, can deepen your connection to the Father and experience healing in the same way.

For many, the pathway to healing the Primal Wound starts with adoption and being brought into a loving family with meaningful relationships that offer new models of trust and intimacy. Similarly, the pathway to healing the Spiritual Primal Wound begins with spiritual adoption into God's family, through which we can be connected once again to God the Father in a powerful and meaningful way.

Adoption in the natural world, as we know it, involves nurturing, healing and integrating a child into a forever family, providing a stable and loving environment. Adoptive families bring healing by helping children address past hurts and trauma, providing emotional and psychological support and modelling unconditional love and acceptance to them to rebuild trust and self-esteem. The new family offers a safe space where the child receives acceptance and can find a sense of belonging and identity. In theory, all of this holds true.

Still, also I know from personal experience the messy, painful and exhausting nature of adoption; more so than any adoptive parents ever bargained for. Adopting a child forces you to confront relational issues and consider your own attachment style. And you often have to fight for joy. In a sermon preached on February 10th 2007, entitled *Adoption The Heart of the Gospel*, John Piper said this about adoption: "Praise God for people ready to embrace the suffering—known and unknown."[2]

He was speaking from personal experience of having adopted himself. He knows, as do we, how we go into adoption with our eyes wide open, knowing there will be challenges and pain along the way. And then it becomes harder, more painful and less rewarding than you thought.

---

2. https://www.desiringgod.org/messages/adoption-the-heart-of-the-gospel

Social services train adoptive parents for the worst-case scenario. But if you want to consider adoption, don't let me put you off. From a Christian point of view, it represents one of the most incredible acts of generosity, grace, selflessness and love you could ever do. As Piper says, "God's cost to adopt us was infinitely greater than any cost we will endure in adopting and raising children."

The cost to Jesus of being part of God's plan to adopt us into his family was outrageous. Our salvation and adoption cost him his life. We read in Isaiah 53:5 (NKJV): "But he was wounded for our transgressions, he was bruised for our iniquities: the chastisement of our peace was upon him; and with his stripes, we are healed." This verse seems highly appropriate within our discussions around the Spiritual Primal Wound. Jesus experienced the spiritual Primal Wound on the cross. He cried out, "My God, My God, why have you forsaken me?" (Matthew 27:46). But there was no answer.

In those moments of God's silence, Jesus was separated from his father for the first and only time ever. He had a profound experience of loss, separation and suffering, which mirrors our understanding and experience of the Fall and the Spiritual Primal Wound. He was wounded for us. We can find healing through being reconnected to the Father through Jesus experiencing the Spiritual Primal Wound for himself.

Adoption in the Roman world and culture

The Bible uses adoption as the framework to help us understand much of what was happening regarding Jesus' death. The Apostle Paul refers to spiritual adoption three times in his letters to the Romans, Galatians and Ephesians. Galatians 4:4-5 says: "When the fullness of time had come, God sent forth his Son, born of woman, born under the law, to redeem those who were under the law, so that we might receive adoption as sons."

When writing about this in the same sermon as noted above, John Piper says:

> The deepest and strongest foundation of adoption is located not in the act of humans adopting humans, but in God adopting humans. And this act is not part of his ordinary providence in the world; it is at the heart of the gospel.

All three audiences Paul wrote to about adoption would have been influenced by Roman culture and familiar with their customs and legal practices. Therefore, I suggest Paul was referring to adoption as understood from a Roman perspective, which may inform our understanding. They understood adoption as carrying a much weightier legal emphasis.

The Greek term used by Paul in his writing means "to place as a son" (Strong's Concordance, Greek 5206). Adoption was a process used to bring predominantly adult males into a family, thereby ensuring succession, either in the absence of an heir or to ensure a suitable heir was in place. For example, Julius Caesar adopted his great-nephew, Augustus, in his will. Augustus went on to become the first Emperor of the Roman Empire.

There was no such corresponding concept or legal process in Jewish culture. They had other legal mechanisms in place, including a provision for the brother of someone deceased to become the head of his household automatically. There are only three references to adoption in the Old Testament, all of which take place in other cultural contexts: Moses (Exodus 2:10), Genubath (1 King 11:20) and Esther (Esther 2:7).

From a Roman perspective, the consequences of adoption were as follows:[3] The family chose the Adoptee; the Adoptee was a new person in the legal sense; they were given a new identity and a new name, and their old debts were cancelled. In addition, while it was legally possible under stringent circumstances to reverse an adoption, it was a formal process with significant legal and social consequences. This option was seldom used, reflecting the seriousness with which Roman society regarded the institution of adoption and family integrity.

Spiritual adoption through Roman eyes

Paul's use of adoption imagery in his writings is clear because Roman adoption closely mirrors spiritual adoption in the New Testament:

- God <u>chose</u> us - Ephesians 1:4-6: "For he chose us in him before the creation of the world to be holy and blameless in his sight. In love he predestined us for adoption to sonship through Jesus Christ, in accordance with his pleasure and will—to the praise of his glorious grace, which he has freely given us in the One he loves." As Ephesians 1:4-6 highlights, God chose believers and predestined them for adoption as his sons and daughters, thereby establishing a foundational sense of self grounded in divine love and acceptance.

- We are a <u>new creation</u>: 2 Corinthians 5:17, "Therefore, if anyone is in Christ, the new creation has come: The old has gone, the new is here!" This spiritual and moral transformation signifies a complete renewal of one's life and character.

---

3. Ellen Mady (Diocese of Pittsburgh), *How the Roman practice of adoption sheds light on what St. Paul was talking about,* article published in Aleteia on 9th December 2017

- We are given a <u>new name</u>: Revelation 2:17b, "I will also give that person a white stone with a new name written on it, known only to the one who receives it."

- Our <u>old debts are cancelled</u>: Colossians 2:14: "Having cancelled the charge of our legal indebtedness, which stood against us and condemned us; he has taken it away, nailing it to the cross." Spiritual adoption involves the forgiveness of sins and redemption through Christ. Colossians 2:14 speaks of the cancellation of the legal charges against believers, signifying the removal of guilt and the establishment of a clean slate with God.

- We belong to a <u>forever family</u>: John 8:35: "Now a slave has no permanent place in the family, but a son belongs to it forever." Spiritual adoption assures believers of their eternal security in God's family. John 8:35 emphasises how a son belongs to the family forever, underscoring the permanence and stability of this relationship with God.

Adoption for Romans and modern society follows a particularly complicated legal process. Spiritual adoption on the other hand proves straightforward. John 1:12 says, "Yet to all who did receive him, to those who believed in his name, he gave the right to become children of God." Galatians 3:26 says: "So in Christ Jesus, you are all children of God through faith." Adoption into the family of God requires simply putting faith in or believing in Jesus Christ. And once adopted into the spiritual family, the benefits are remarkable:

- Freedom from slavery: "The Spirit you received does not make you slaves, so that you live in fear again; rather, the Spirit you received brought about your adoption to sonship. And by him we cry, 'Abba, Father'." (Romans 8:15).

- The Receiving of the Holy Spirit (Romans 8:15).

- An intimate relationship with God the Father (Romans 8:15). Abba, as previously referenced, signifies a close, personal and affectionate relationship similar to that of a child with their parent, offering comfort and security.

- An inheritance as co-heirs with Christ, "Now if we are children, then we are heirs—heirs of God and co-heirs with Christ, if indeed we share in his sufferings in order that we may also share in his glory."(Romans 8:17)

- Future glory and resurrection, "Not only so, but we ourselves, who have the firstfruits of the Spirit, groan inwardly as we wait eagerly for our adoption to sonship, the redemption of our bodies." (Romans 8: v 23)

Adoption as a means of connection to the Father

Paul's writings suggest that adoption in the New Testament should be understood like Roman adoption. Paul emphasises security, inheritance and the cancelling of our debts. Yet, Jesus also identified with us in taking on the Spiritual Primal Wound for himself so we might be adopted into the family of God. Spiritual adoption includes aspects of natural adoption, like healing through connection as part of an ongoing process.

Adoption happens in a moment. In natural adoption, a judge approves it. In spiritual adoption, God, who judges and rules over everything, gives his seal of approval. Then healing can begin.

As an adoptive dad, I know it takes time to connect with my adopted children. Me connecting with them or for them connecting with me proves challenging. This process includes removing roadblocks, clearing the way and helping them lay the foundations of the pathways in their brains leading to healthy boundaries, autonomy and connected relationships.

The same applies to spiritual adoption. The adoption process itself is simple and relatively straightforward. We reconnect to the Father through his son, Jesus. Once the connection has been established, the healing process can begin. Healing will likely take both time and hard work. Remember how God sticks with you for the long haul and has a plan. We can together have hope for change. We can be "renewed by the transformation of our minds."

As we embrace the transformative power of spiritual adoption, we uncover a path not just to legal redemption but also to profound relational healing. Similarly to how foster carers and adopters are guided to nurture through therapeutic parenting, God employs divine therapeutic parenting to mend our spiritual and emotional wounds. These heavenly parenting principles can profoundly shape and heal our relationships.

Prayer

Whoever dwells in the shelter of the Most High
will rest in the shadow of the Almighty.
I will say of the Lord, 'He is my refuge and my fortress,
my God, in whom I trust.'
Psalm 91:1-2

Abba, Father, thank you for adopting us into your family. Thank you that through the life, death and resurrection of Jesus, we can be connected to you and enjoy relationship with our Creator. Transform our hearts and minds as we embrace fully our new identity in You. Fill our hearts with the truth that we now belong to a forever family and that security and safety are found in you. Help us to release the fears and insecurities binding us, and to accept your love and grace.

In Jesus' name. Amen.

Chapter 9

God's Healing Touch for the Child Who Hurts

Regardless of our background, we all have a spiritual primal wound because of the Fall. As a therapeutic parent, God heals this wound and brings us closer to him. He brings a healing touch to all who are hurting. You may be experiencing pain yourself. You likely long to experience healing through connection to the Father for yourself.

Adoption in the natural provides a context to explore how God heals the spiritual primal wound. Children who are adopted know especially well what this pain feels like. Whether it be as a result of the "primal wound" from being abandoned or the terrible things that happened to them, all adopted children are hurting somewhere. To assist them in processing their pain and the resulting emotions, professionals recommend an approach known as Therapeutic Parenting. As we consider the principles of Therapeutic Parenting, we will quickly see how God uses the same ones in how he relates to us as our heavenly father.

Therapeutic Parenting

An adoptive parent offers love, support and stability to help the child feel safe and heal from past hurts. This task presents a challenge, considering what many adopted children have endured. The responsibility lies with the parents to make it as easy as possible for the child to connect and start healing.

Therapeutic Parenting offers a profoundly nurturing and empathetic approach seeking to address the child's emotional and psychological needs. This method focuses on consistent, compassionate and tailored responses to a child's distress and behaviour. This consistent care allows the child to begin to get control of their emotions and understand their actions. Sarah Naish, an adoptive mum and best-selling author, known for her work on Therapeutic Parenting, says this:

> The aim of Therapeutic Parenting is to enable the child to recover from the trauma they have experienced. This is done by developing new pathways in the child's brain to help them to link cause and effect, reduce their levels of fear and shame and to help them start to make sense of their world[1].

Therapeutic Parenting contrasts sharply with traditional methods. Your own experiences as a parent or being parented may vary greatly. Therapeutic Parenting doesn't focus on punishing the child using verbal reprimands, timeouts and physical discipline. No-one places an expectation on the child to feel or express remorse or empathy.

Instead, Therapeutic Parenting focuses on creating a safe and predictable environment where children can thrive. Carers establish boundaries and routines not as forms of control but as anchors of trust and safety. These routines aim to help build the pathways in the child's brain which lead to an understanding of cause and effect. Visual aids, like timetables, can support this sense of consistency, making daily life more reliable and reassuring. Within this structure, carers steep their responses to a child's needs in empathy, using

---

1. Sarah Neish, *The A-Z of Therapeutic Parenting*, (Jessica Kingsley Publishers, 2018)

Playfulness, Acceptance, Curiosity and Empathy (the PACE model) to connect with and guide the child.

If the carers did not meet these specific emotional connections and reciprocity needs early on, this must be rectified within the context of these new relationships. However, Therapeutic Parenting isn't just useful for adopted children or children who have additional needs. All children alike may benefit, leading to deeper reciprocal connection. God uses similar principles in how he cares for us as his children because he knows what we need to get better connected to him. He promotes an environment in which transformative healing can take place. He provides unconditional love, healing and restoration, divine guidance and discipline, empathy and understanding and a profound sense of belonging.

Unconditional love

The Bible makes it clear that God loves us unconditionally and unwaveringly. John 3:16 says, "For God so loved the world that he gave his one and only Son, that whoever believes in him shall not perish but have eternal life." God loves us not based on merits or deeds. His love does not depend on past hurts or current struggles. He loves us because he loves us. This establishes the secure base from which we can explore, grow and return, knowing we are always welcomed and cherished, no matter what.

If you have an insecure attachment style, there are several reasons why you might find it hard to accept God's love as truly unconditional:

- You may have developed trust issues as a result of not being able to trust your primary caregiver.

- You may be convinced you are unlovable and not deserving of God's love because of how low your self-esteem is.

- You may be emotionally distant, hindering you from engaging with just how much and how unconditionally God loves you.

- Your parents may have loved you conditionally, or you may have perceived it to be conditional. This may have predisposed you to believe all love comes with criteria and led you to develop conditions of worth.

- You may believe God could withdraw his love if you fail to meet expectations or make mistakes.

Hopefully, you have experienced unconditional love at some point in your life. Looking back, I wonder how it affected your actions and sense of security?

Healing and restoration

Restoration and healing flow throughout the Bible, in both the Old and New Testaments. Healing defines God's nature and his plan for his people. The Father, Son and Spirit all engage in the work of healing. God is named "Jehovah Rapha," meaning "the Lord who heals" (Exodus 15:26). In the New Testament, Jesus announces the kingdom is near and confirms it through signs, wonders and many healings. Paul, in his letter to the Corinthians, highlights the Spirit's gift of healing to God's people (1 Cor 12:9).

One story of healing from Luke 8 may help develop this further. A woman, suffering with bleeding for twelve years, touches the hem of Jesus' cloak and receives instant healing. Jesus, realising power has gone out from him, asks, "Who touched me?" The woman eventually owns up and Jesus responds by calling her "daughter" and telling her how her faith has made her well. This involves much more than physical healing; it's a story of complete restoration.

Given the nature of her issue, the woman was considered unclean and was consequently a social and religious outcast. She must have been feeling some shame as a result of her condition. In addition, only a family member was allowed to touch the hem of Jesus' garment. By admitting to touching him, she was risking humiliation and possibly even punishment. And yet Jesus responded with grace, empathy and compassion. By calling her daughter, he validated her actions in touching the hem of his robe. He restored her to her community. He washed away years of shame and isolation. She went on to be an example for many who "begged him to let them touch even the edge of his cloak, and all who touched it were healed" (Mark 6:56).

Jesus is both healer and restorer, caring for physical, psychological and emotional well-being. He healed this woman physically and forged an intimate connection by calling her "daughter." He removed her shame and restored her to her community. While touching Jesus' robe brought physical healing, connecting with him brought healing and restoration in every other aspect of her life.

Embracing Jesus as a healer and connecting to the Father through him leads to spiritual renewal and transformation in every area of our lives. Jesus came to bring life to the full (John 10:10). Fullness of life is not about survival. Fullness involves thriving in every possible way. This woman was restored to the fullness of life. I have hope you, too, can be made whole again, healed and restored through God's healing touch.

> **Pause for thought**
>
> Consider setting aside some time to think about this now.
>
> - Do you see areas in your life where you need healing?
>
> Ask the Holy Spirit to help you discern exactly what you need. Then ask Jesus to help you to start the healing process through connecting you to the Father.

Guidance and discipline

Connection before correction constitutes one of the fundamental principles of Therapeutic Parenting. This principle was drummed into us during adoption training, and it has stuck with us. Whatever form the correction takes, it comes from a place of reaffirming love first and foremost. I mentioned before about my friend who was surprised when her godson's mother hugged him and told him she loved him after she had disciplined him. Well, this takes matters one step further. The hug and the affirmation of love come before any correction. God acts towards us in the same way. Hebrews 12:6 says, "Because the Lord disciplines the one he loves, and he chastens everyone he accepts as his son." God's discipline connects directly to love and sonship.

The meaning of the term discipline differs from what first comes to mind. Author L. R. Knost points us in the direction of a different meaning altogether:

> Here's the thing, effective parenting and, more specifically, effective discipline, don't require punishment. Equating discipline with punishment is an unfortunate, but common misconception. The root word in discipline is actually disciple which in the verb form means to guide, lead, teach, model and encourage. In the noun form disciple means one who embraces the teaching of, follows the example of and models their life after[2].

God's discipline should be viewed within the context of divine guidance and encouragement. His discipline expresses his love. He disciplines us to guide us in paths of righteousness. God purposefully and constructively, seeks to mature us in character, encouraging our growth and producing positive change.

Take the example of timeouts and the so-called naughty step. Therapeutic Parenting discourages their use because these forms of discipline may tap into a whole host of negative feelings for the child who has previously been neglected. Instead, carers connect with the child using time-in to assist them in calming their emotions and restoring a sense of order.

As Christians, when we have done something wrong, we often mistakenly feel as though we need to be punished. We self-impose a form of purgatory, very much like the naughty step because we think God should act towards us accordingly. This is not biblical. His discipline never involves punishment. Nowhere in scripture do we get the sense God wants to punish his children.

---

2. L.R. Knost, *The Gentle Parent: Positive, Practical, Effective Discipline*, (Little Hearts Books, 2013)

The punishment we deserved was placed on Jesus instead. Isaiah 53:5: "...the punishment that brought us peace was on him..." So, instead of pushing us away, God wants to draw us closer to him to teach, guide and lead us to work out how to do better next time. He does this best from a place of deeper connection. Maybe next time you feel you need a timeout, remember this and see if you can press into God rather than pull away.

Again, it may be hard for you to get your head around this. You may have had negative past experiences with authority figures who punished you a lot. You may have lived in fear of what was going to happen next. You may not have experienced connection after correction, let alone connection before correction. So often authority figures and how they acted towards us shaped our view of God. Those perceptions may not be easy to shake. You may struggle to align your thinking with what the Bible says.

As you reflect on God's discipline, can you think of a time when you faced a difficult situation? Are there ways in which it led to personal growth or more profound understanding?

Empathy and understanding

Healing attachment issues requires empathy because it forms the foundation for understanding, connection and trust. Empathy validates an individual's experiences and feelings, allowing them to feel loved and valued. The Bible reveals that Jesus, God made man, experienced the full range of human emotions—joy, sorrow, hunger, grief and pain. He understands what it means to be human, face temptation and struggle because He has walked that path with us. Hebrews 4:15 states, "Jesus sympathises with our weaknesses and was tempted in every way yet was without sin." Throughout his ministry, Jesus acted out of empathy and compassion for human suffering, feeding the hungry, healing the sick, freeing captives and raising the dead.

Empathy plays an essential role because shame often overwhelms those struggling with insecure attachment styles, and empathy serves as the antidote to shame.

Brené Brown, an American professor and author renowned for her work on shame, explains this concept well. She says:

> If we're going to find our way back to each other, we have to understand and know empathy, because empathy's the antidote to shame. If you put shame in a Petri dish, it needs three things to grow exponentially: secrecy, silence and judgement. If you put the same amount of shame in a Petri dish and douse it with empathy, it can't survive. The two most powerful words when we're in struggle: me too[3].

---

3. Brené Brown Ted Talk, 16/03/2012, *Listening to Shame*

Pause for thought

Shame exerts a powerful influence over us. Reading about shame and how it thrives in secrecy, silence and judgement may provoke a strong response in you. If it does, then this may be one of those toxic thoughts we talked about identifying. You may need to sit with the painful feelings to determine why you feel that way about yourself.

Or it may be something you could talk about with a friend, should you feel comfortable doing so. The tools identified help you reframe those negative thoughts and feelings to make you feel good about yourself again.

- Can you remember a time when someone showed you empathy? How did their understanding impact your feelings of worth and connection?

- How do you typically respond to feelings of shame? Do you notice patterns or coping mechanisms?

- How do you feel about seeking support from others, including God, to address these feelings?

- Do you find it challenging to open up emotionally or ask for help?

If you have an insecure attachment style, you may struggle to open up emotionally or ask for help. Opening up about your pain can be terrifying. The fear of being misunderstood or judged can make you retreat into isolation. I know how overwhelming it can be to feel disconnected, as if no one truly understands the depth of your pain. But you are not alone in this. By embracing vulnerability, you take the first step toward true connection and healing. The healing process requires us to reach out to God and others. Opening up requires a level of vulnerability, but when you make yourself vulnerable and are not met with judgement, you may learn you are not as bad as you may have thought. God always meets us where we are, taking our unique needs, attachment issues and styles into account as he seeks to connect with us to bring healing.

Adoption and belonging

Within the context of adoption, we commonly talk about a "forever family". This expression confirms to the child that they will not be moved about again. They have been placed in a permanent family, for better or for worse. Only some people like the use of this term because, sadly, sometimes adoption placements do break down. In our context, the expression proves helpful because, with God, there is a genuine sense of permanence. Once you have been adopted into the family, he will be faithful to you until the end. Nothing you do can separate you from his love. Nothing you do will make him love you any more or any less.

Let me be clear: I am coming at this from the point of view of God's faithfulness. He will not let you down. He does not change his mind, and, as far as it depends on him, once he has adopted you, you remain part of the family for all eternity. With this comes a profound sense of identity and belonging, a crucial part of the healing process. Do you think knowing how secure you are in God the Father impacts your life and relationships?

The Parable of the Prodigal Son

The parable of the prodigal son illustrates many of these considerations, albeit the parable speaks much more about the father than the son. In a nutshell, the parable of the prodigal son tells the story of a young man who demands his inheritance, leaves home and squanders it all. Destitute and remorseful, he returns to his father, who welcomes him back with open arms, celebrating his return. Meanwhile, the elder brother feels jealous and resentful. Still, the father reassures him of his love and the importance of celebrating his brother's return.

The father's actions and attitudes in the parable of the prodigal son reveal his deep commitment to fostering reciprocal connections with his sons. He demonstrates unconditional love by welcoming the prodigal son back into the family, even after the son has squandered his entire inheritance. The son's worth does not depend on his actions, but on his identity as a son. This provides a secure base from which the son can explore the world and a safe haven to return to, no matter what he has lost. The father's acceptance comes without judgement; he always welcomes his son back with open arms. The father shows profound empathy and understanding by not condemning his son but instead being filled with compassion when he returns.

The father has been watching and waiting for his son's return and when he finally sees him, he runs to greet him. This act is significant because men of his age and status did not typically run. By doing so, he risks bringing shame upon himself. He runs to reach his son before anyone else in the village can, knowing they would seek to shame the son for wasting his inheritance. The father takes this shame upon himself to protect his son from it.

Additionally, the father forgives unconditionally. He celebrates his son's return with a grand party, rejoicing now he has found his lost son. He also takes the time to reassure his other son, who struggles with jealousy and insecurity following his brother's return. The father shows him just how inclusive and abundant his love is. This incredible story illustrates how God the Father acts towards us despite our rebellion and sin. God demonstrates how his love, empathy and forgiveness are always available to us, offering a secure base and a safe haven for our return.

God offers a secure base and a safe haven, never leaving or forsaking us. We need not fear separation from him, as his presence surrounds us everywhere. His goodness remains constant. All His actions uplift, empower and encourage, guiding our growth. In every way, He exemplifies the perfect parent. Nicky Gumble reflects on this in the Bible with Nicky and Pippa Gumble (day 59) when he says:

> God is such a parent. His faithfulness is without question. His generosity is perfect. His affection is tender and loving. His presence is permanent. His acceptance of you is unconditional. His communication is up-building and for your best interest. His authority is right and true.

As a two-way street, attachment requires a strong connection from both parties to form a secure bond. There are some practical things we can do to engage with the connection from our point of view and ensure genuine reciprocity. We can see real transformation and healing in our lives.

Prayer

Isaiah 40:11: "He tends his flock like a shepherd: He gathers the lambs in his arms and carries them close to his heart; he gently leads those that have young."

Abba, Father, embrace us with your healing love. Guide us, lead us, teach us, nurture us and restore us. Let us feel your presence in our daily lives and find peace and wholeness in your care.

In Jesus' name, Amen.

Chapter 10

Reclaiming Inner Healing and Wholeness Through Cultivating Divine Intimacy

God reaches out to us with his healing embrace. By cultivating a deep, intimate relationship with him from our perspective, we can reclaim inner healing and wholeness. Certain practices and attitudes foster a closer connection with God, helping you to experience profound healing, peace and a renewed sense of wholeness.

Foundations of grace

Grace forms the foundation of our relationship with God. He gives his love and favour towards us freely and unconditionally. We do nothing to earn his love, favour or blessing. Ephesians 2:8-9 states, "For it is by grace you have been saved, through faith—and this is not from yourselves, it is the gift of God—not by works, so that no one can boast." His grace sustains our relationship, not our efforts or worth.

Yet, we have also highlighted many times how forming reciprocal relationships is a two-way street. The secure bond we form with our creator requires a response from us of obedience and trust, dependence on him and returning to him as our safe haven. God's grace provides us with a secure base and a safe haven. At the same time, our response to his grace plays a crucial role in maintaining and deepening the relationship.

God's grace assures us of his presence and care for us. He says in Hebrews 13:5: "Never will I leave you; never will I forsake you." Our understanding of this can transform how we approach him, moving us from a place of fear or striving to one of trust and rest. The reality does not change, yet our perception of his presence and care wavers. Not feeling his presence can impact how we relate to him.

I am currently looking for work and need to find a job imminently. I know what the Bible tells me about the Lord being my provider (Jehovah Jireh) and how he has a good plan. Yet still, I find myself at times, wanting to wake Jesus up since he appears to be sleeping in the boat to ask him, "Don't you care if we drown?" God remains good and faithful. I am nervous and a little afraid. This impacts our relationship.

While grace means that God's love does not depend on me, a thriving relationship does depend on my active participation. Like in any mutual relationship, where both parties actively seek to stay close, my relationship with God flourishes when I seek him, communicate through prayer and align my life with his will and teachings. I do not seek to earn his love but I do reciprocate the relationship he initiates.

It takes two to tango

Parents may relate to this through their own experiences with their children. You might be doing everything possible to promote an atmosphere where the relationship can flourish. You may be endlessly playing attachment tennis, trying to do everything in a way that gives your child or children every opportunity to connect with you. And yet something needs to be clicking—not because you have done anything wrong. Your child does not seem able to connect with you on some level at this point. God always brings the same patience, tolerance and perseverance you need with your children, to his relationship with us.

The bond between a caregiver and a child resembles a dance. And yes, it does take two to tango. In a harmonious dance, where both partners attune to each other and move gracefully, both play an active role. The Lord leads, guides, initiates the steps and oversees the transitions. We follow his leadership and cues. The coming together of the two necessitates clear communication. Then something beautiful comes out of it.

The essential element of connection lies at the core of every nurturing parent-child dynamic. The relationship that forms goes beyond just emotion. Forging a profound emotional bond between parent and child, or between creator and created, requires deliberate effort. Spiritual adoption into God's family ignites this transformative process, allowing us to call God 'Abba Father.' It provides a new identity, a sense of security, acceptance and significance, addressing our fears of rejection and abandonment. Being brought into a relationship with God opens up the possibility of experiencing healing through connection to him.

Spiritual practices such as prayer, meditation, reflective journaling and participating in a faith community can deepen our connection. They help us to be aware of his presence, leading and guiding. They can give us space to process our emotional turmoil and past hurts. Integrating modern psychology with spiritual practices and disciplines offers a holistic approach to deepening intimacy with God. By embracing concepts from both fields, individuals can foster a more profound spiritual connection, heal from past traumas and cultivate a secure relationship with God. Healing comes through connection to the Father.

What follows are some ways to help you be more responsive to God's grace in your life, bringing more incredible healing.

Establish a daily routine in mindfulness and prayer

Our brains have an incredible capacity for learning. Repeating the same task regularly helps the brain form pathways. As an infant, those pathways are formed through the endless repetition of the cycle of connection. The infant expresses need and then responds to the fact the need has been met. The same holds true of our relationship with our Creator. In Philippians 4:6, the Bible tells us to "not be anxious about anything, but in every situation, by prayer and petition, with thanksgiving, present your requests to God." Prayer enables essential communication with God and expression of our needs. When the disciples asked Jesus to teach them how to pray, he responded by giving them what we now know as the Lord's Prayer:

> Our Father in heaven, hallowed be your name, your kingdom come, your will be done, on earth as it is in heaven. Give us today our daily bread. And forgive us our debts, as we also have forgiven our debtors. And lead us not into temptation, but deliver us from the evil one. (Matthew 6:9-13)

Prayer can be complex and confusing. There are no straightforward answers as to how to pray. The Bible seems to contradict itself at times with how prayer works, probably because it never works as a formula but rather a conversation with God who loves me, is for me and wants the best for me. The Lord's Prayer begins with the same expression of intimacy and connection we considered when thinking about spiritual adoption: "Abba, Father." This prayer focuses on connecting with God in a personal and intimate way. And not just any God. A good God, who wants to do me good and will do me good. Late pastor and author Tim Keller said:

> Prayer is both conversation and encounter with God... We must know the awe of praising his glory, the intimacy of finding his grace, and the struggle of asking his help, all of which can lead us to know the spiritual reality of his presence.[1]

Prayer is a conversation with a God who sees the whole picture when we can only see a piece of it. He's sovereign, all-powerful, and His perspective is bigger than ours. That's why prayer doesn't start with asking for things. It starts with recognising who He is, honouring His name, seeking His kingdom, and trusting His will. That changes everything. When we remember that God is good, that He knows what we don't, and that He's both a secure foundation and a safe refuge, it reshapes how we pray. We don't have to come desperate, like we're trying to twist His arm. We can come confident, knowing that whether He answers right away or asks us to keep praying and waiting, He's going to give us what's best. Tim Keller, in his book on prayer, puts it this way

> "God will either give us what we ask or give us what we would have asked if we knew everything he knows."

In this way of praying, we express trust and submission which we identified as being traits of secure attachment. Trust manifests itself in a dependence on God for our daily bread. He is Jehovah Jireh - the Lord is my provider. We turn to him when we are in need knowing he will meet our needs. Jesus tells us not to worry in Matthew 6:8 because "your Father knows what you need even before you ask him." He provides both a secure base and a safe haven. He can be trusted to lead us and guide us. He will "deliver us

---

1. Timothy Keller, *Prayer: Experiencing Awe and Intimacy with God* (Dutton)

from evil". Psychologically, mindfulness and prayer assist in getting better control of your emotions and helping you to feel less anxious. Spiritually, they foster a greater awareness of God's presence and openness to his leading and guidance.

Engage with scripture prayerfully, focusing on connection

Psalm 23 typifies a 'psalm of attachment' because it describes our deep personal connection to God the Father. Similarly, we could also speak of the Lord's Prayer as a prayer of attachment because it directs us to pray in a way that deepens our connection to him. Similar considerations can be found in many other parts of scripture. You may want to read through passages you identify with to meditate on your connection to the Father. Find passages related to God's fatherly love, care and protection. As you read, consider how these words convey God's role as a secure base and a safe haven, much like a caregiver. Meditate on the words, imagining yourself safe and secure in the arms of the Father. Deuteronomy 33:27 says: "The eternal God is your refuge, and underneath are the everlasting arms." You may even want to picture yourself being held by God.

British artist and illustrator Charlie Mackesy, best known for his work *The Boy, the Mole, the Fox and the Horse* designed one of my wife's favourite pieces of artwork. The image entitled *Held*, depicts one person holding another closely in their arms and the person being held, snuggling in. We are poignantly reminded through this image of the power of human connection. We all, without exception, need support, the comfort of being held and the strength of vulnerability and compassion. Held reflects a visual narrative that encourages empathy, kindness and the nurturing of meaningful relationships. You may wish to find this image online and use it to imagine your connection to God. As you do so, you could focus on slowing your breathing and physically relaxing. This in and of itself can help to soothe the nervous system, reduce anxiety levels and increase your awareness of connection to yourself and God.

> **Pause for thought**
>
> You could begin a meditation on scripture with passages like Psalm 23 and the Lord's Prayer and use what we have learned to think about how you connect with God and to think about his presence. Read through the passage. Meditate on it. Pray over it. Contemplate its application to your life, particularly thinking about your connection to him. Ask yourself:
>
> - How do these passages relate to your life now?
>
> - In what ways do you feel God's presence as you engage with these scriptures?
>
> - How can the themes of trust, provision and guidance in these scriptures shape your understanding of God's role in your life?
>
> - What new insights about your personal narrative and relationship with God emerge from this meditation?
>
> From a psychological point of view, this promotes open-mindedness and can lead to a new understanding of your personal narrative and story. From a spiritual perspective, it helps deepen your understanding of scripture, bringing a greater awareness of God's loving character.

Reflective journaling

You could then transition into journaling or praying, using your time to communicate openly with God and sharing your thoughts, feelings and desires. You could make note of any areas where you particularly struggle with insecure attachment and how your insecure tendencies affect your relationship with God. For some people, writing out their prayers and thoughts focuses the mind and makes their spiritual life more intentional, helping them to articulate their thoughts and feelings to God more clearly. Keeping a journal may also be an opportunity to record prayers and the answers received. Reviewing a record of past answers to prayers presents a great way to build faith when facing a challenging situation in the present or the future.

This kind of vulnerability can bring an emotional release as you voice your deepest fears, anxieties and pain. From a psychological perspective, it helps to increase self-awareness, emotional processing and acceptance of your flaws and struggles. From a spiritual point of view, it encourages discernment and deeper insight into your spiritual journey, an essential part of the healing process. As you acknowledge and bring your brokenness before the Lord, he can bind up your wounds. Psalm 34:18 says, "The LORD is near to the broken-hearted and saves the crushed in spirit."

Facing your inner gremlins

Journalling might only be for some. If you learn through reading and writing, journalling will work for you. But if, like me, you prefer a more hands-on approach including physical activity, you may wish to take a different approach. You are still seeking to find a way to face your inner gremlins, which may be getting in the way of you connecting on a deeper level with God.

I went for a walk by the canal a few years ago. I find prayer walking, reflective walking and getting out in nature with God benefit me mentally, physically and spiritually. On this occasion, I used the time to allow my deepest fears and struggles to express themselves. I had been reading some work by Christian neuroscientist Dr Caroline Leaf and loosely followed something she had recommended. This involved listening as my fears talked at me for almost half an hour. During the whole time, I did not rationalise or respond. I just let them talk until, as far as I knew, they had nothing more to say. Often, when we begin to think about our fears, anxieties, or hurts, we stop midway. The fear of the unknown can become more significant than the reality itself. If you allow yourself to sit with your deepest fears, anxiety and pain (either on your own or with help if needed), it will enable you to face and acknowledge your difficulties, discomforts and emotional baggage without avoidance or denial. You can confront your inner gremlins.

Psychologically, making these connections can lead to increased self-awareness as you become more conscious of the narratives you tell yourself. The process encourages you to deal with your emotions instead of suppressing them, leading to better-managing stress and anxiety. Confronting difficult situations and feelings also encourages you to build mental and emotional resilience. From a spiritual point of view, you may feel better connected with yourself and empowered to grow in maturity. You may have more compassion for others as you embrace your struggles, and ultimately, you should experience a greater depth of inner peace.

Account-ability

During my canal walk, I made dictation notes on my phone and nervously shared these unedited notes with trusted friends to bring light into dark places. Putting yourself out there in this way takes courage. Sharing with and opening up to the right people, your people, is also essential. You want to be sure these people won't be judgemental but will respond to you with empathy, compassion and understanding. You also hope they will bring an element of challenge, encouraging and holding you accountable for your ability.

God then started to speak to me about how he wanted to respond to what had been said. There was such a sense of affirmation of calling and belonging in what he said to me. I may have come as close as I have to experiencing first-hand "the peace of God, which transcends all understanding" (Philippians 4:7). We so often tend to keep these things hidden away in deep places. Shame thrives in an environment of secrecy, silence and judgement. On the contrary, as we bring these things into the light through open, honest and vulnerable communication with Abba, Father, and others, we deprive shame of the oxygen it needs to survive. Bringing things to the surface that may have been buried deep for a long time can be painful. At the same time, it allows the Father to deal with them, bringing relief and healing.

Actively pursue forgiveness

Forgiveness constitutes another essential element of experiencing healing through connection to the Father. We reflected earlier on the Lord's Prayer as a prayer of attachment. In the middle, it contains this line: "Forgive us our sins, as we forgive those who sin against us." If we want to be forgiven, then we must also forgive. Having a relationship with God requires receiving his forgiveness. Sin gets in the way of us connecting to the Father. Jesus had to die to take away our sins so we might be adopted into God's family.

But also, on an ongoing basis, we must pursue forgiveness from God, keeping a short account and we must pursue forgiving others. This should involve meditation, prayer and, where possible, reconciliation (though, as we have already noted, this does not always solely depend on you). In Ephesians 4:31-32, we read: "Get rid of all bitterness, rage and anger, brawling and slander, along with every form of malice. Be kind and compassionate to one another, forgiving each other, just as in Christ God forgave you."

Holding onto grudges can lead to bitterness and create barriers in our relationship with God. Forgiveness fosters trust, openness, kindness and compassion, all traits of a secure attachment style. From a psychological perspective, forgiveness contributes to emotional and relational healing. From a spiritual point of view, it reflects the very heart of the Gospel. Our forgiveness mirrors the forgiveness God has so graciously given to us.

Participate in a spiritual community

Some aspects of our healing journey are personal. They are born out of prayer, meditation, reflection, journaling and walking with God. We have explored others, such as accountability and forgiveness, which require others to be involved. Actively participating in spiritual community with others instead of going it alone, forms another essential element of connection with God. Hebrews 10:24-25 says: "And let us consider how we may spur one another on toward love and good deeds, not giving up meeting together, as some are in the habit of doing, but encouraging one another—and all the more as you see the Day approaching." Within the context of spiritual community, journeying together, we can encourage one another and build each other up (1 Thessalonians 5:11) We can carry each other's burdens (Galatians 6:2). We can grow and build each other up in love (Ephesians 4:15-16). We can love one another as Jesus commanded (John 13:34).

Experiencing meaningful relationships that offer new models of trust and intimacy moves us towards earned secure attachment. We find these relationships by taking part in a spiritual community. For those with disrupted or insecure early relationships, a loving community can help restore trust and provide a better emotional experience, reflecting God's unconditional love and acceptance.

The community also promotes the whole person's well-being through an integration of spiritual and social support. As we look after each other and love one another in specific and practical ways, it may help to build those pathways in the brain that promote a more profound sense of connection to the Father. From a psychological point of view, being part of a community builds a network of support and reduces feelings of isolation and loneliness. From a spiritual point of view, it encourages fellowship and promotes the outworking of our faith in relationship with others.

Seek therapeutic support aligned with your spiritual values

Sometimes, a personal journey of reflection, prayer and discovery of self, even coupled with the support of a loving community of like-minded people, does not suffice. You may have identified some deep-seated issues about how you related to your parents and how you now relate to God and others. You may also have experienced some terrible things that happened to you as a child. Some people are specially trained to handle these struggles with sensitivity and care. Reaching out for help and seeking the input of a therapist may prove beneficial. Ideally, this would be one who respects and integrates your spiritual beliefs and faith into the therapeutic process. They may guide you on your journey of healing from past wounds and help you get better connected to God the Father in the process.

My wife and I have been doing therapy for the last 6 months to help us build lasting bonds of trust and security with each other and our adopted children. Our therapist has been amazing. She has encouraged me to reason less and feel more. Reflecting on my childhood has taken me to painful places I had not previously accessed in terms of how they made me feel. I've had to bring some of this in prayer to the Lord, questioning why he allowed events which have had such a significant long-term impact. I am learning to bring these matters to him and allow him to minister to me.

This self-reflection has also made me rethink my love languages and what helps me feel connected and loved. I was previously sure my primary love language was acts of service. However, I now realise how performance and achievement were my coping strategies growing up. I had internalised a "condition of worth". I learned that if I achieved well, I felt valued, appreciated and good about myself. My experience led me to equate acts of service with love.

Recently, I was feeling very low one night, and my wife leaned over and snuggled up next to me. I felt more connected and loved in that moment than ever, which surprised me. As I connected with my deeper feelings, I longed for more physical affection. This realisation has led me to reach out more regarding giving and receiving love through physical contact with my wife and children. Consequently, I feel more loved, appreciated and connected to my family.

Since attachment is a two-way street, this change in behaviour impacts them too. My daughter comes across as very tactile and adores squeezy hugs. My son seems to appreciate feeling physically close to me, and there had been many times when Rach had sought to snuggle up to me and I had resisted. I had been trying to connect with people through a learned behaviour rather than based on my natural inclination. This dynamic led to disconnection and confusion and for a long time, left me feeling lonely.

This journey toward healing through connection to the Father challenges us, often bringing pain that signals deeper issues needing attention. Addressing pain becomes essential in the healing process, which rarely follows a straightforward path. Healing typically brings periods of increased discomfort as underlying issues surface. However, pushing through these challenges opens the door to spiritual growth and a deeper connection with God the Father.

We must recognise that cultivating divine intimacy is an ongoing journey. You have not reached the end destination; instead, this point represents the middle of your journey, another chapter in the story of your life written by God. The practices and perspectives we've discussed are tools to help you draw closer to God, allowing his love to heal and restore you. As you continue to nurture this relationship, you'll find deeper peace and a more profound sense of wholeness. Jesus cultivated intimacy with his Abba throughout his life on earth. He found strength, courage and comfort from closeness to his dad. So as we near the end of this conversation together, what better place to finish than considering the impact of Jesus' relationship to God and how much it sustained him in everything he did.

Prayer

> Jeremiah 29:13: "You will seek me and find me when you seek me with all your heart."

Abba, Father, draw us ever closer to you. Cultivate in us a deep and intimate relationship with you, where we can share our hearts and hear yours. Let our lives be a reflection of your love and may our connection with you grow stronger and stronger.

In Jesus' name. Amen.

Chapter 11

Jesus' perfect connection to God the Father

Throughout this journey, we have explored the concept of attachment and how it relates to our early bonds with our caregivers and our relationship with God, our ultimate caregiver. Jesus typifies the perfect example of secure attachment to God the Father. His example can inspire, guide and empower our spiritual journeys.

Fully divine and fully human

We naturally perceive Jesus as unique, given his divine status as the Son of God, and rightly so. As Paul states in Philippians 2:9-11, "Therefore God exalted him to the highest place and gave him the name that is above every name, that at the name of Jesus, every knee should bow, in heaven and on earth and under the earth, and every tongue acknowledge that Jesus Christ is Lord, to the glory of God the Father." This divine status sets Jesus apart from us, and he is undeniably holy, deserving of our awe, reverence and worship.

Yet, Jesus did not cling to his divine privileges in his earthly life. As Paul also writes in Philippians 2:6-7, "Who, being in very nature God, did not consider equality with God something to be used to his own advantage; rather, he made himself nothing by taking the very nature of a servant, being made in human likeness." Jesus laid aside his divine prerogatives and fully embraced human nature, experiencing all the vulnerabilities and challenges that come with it.

This humility and willingness to become fully human make Jesus deeply relatable. He was born as a helpless baby to Mary and Joseph, forming early bonds with his caregivers. Away in a Manager, the famous Carol suggests that as a newborn, Jesus did not cry. Yet, crying forms a natural and healthy part of the process of expressing need and bonding with the people looking after you. Crying has its place in the cycle of attachment.

Early connection to his earthly parents

Jesus had to form a relationship of trust and intimacy with his parents, the same way we all do. As did they. Attachment is always a two-way street. Mary and Joseph had to connect to their son in the same way he had to connect to them. By crying he let them know he had a need, like being hungry. This two-way nature of attachment reflects the reciprocity in our relationship with God, where he also seeks our connection and trust. This may well have been complicated for Joseph. He was not Jesus' biological father. Mary became pregnant through the Holy Spirit while she was still a virgin. Joseph planned to call off the engagement quietly, but he was visited by an Angel who told him what the plan was. He accepted his role as Jesus' earthly father. He effectively adopted Jesus and loved him as his own.

The circumstances of Jesus' birth were not ideal either, and not long after, his whole family had to flee to Egypt as refugees to avoid Jesus being killed by Herod's soldiers. Jesus' traumatic early years are further evidence he went through many of the life challenges we have experienced as well. Yet, he was able to overcome them with resilience and emotional strength. This reminds us of the Old Testament story of Joseph. Joseph's early secure attachment to Jacob enabled him to persevere and succeed despite numerous challenges. Joseph's journey showcased a secure attachment style, marked by his ability to form healthy relationships, maintain emotional stability and trust God's plan.

The same proves true of Jesus. His father Joseph's protective action and acceptance of his son gave Jesus an early secure base. Joseph communicated his unconditional love for Jesus, for whom he provided a family, security and acceptance. Jesus learned much from his earthly father, including his trade as a carpenter. They would likely have spent much time together learning the trade and bonding over the family business. Joseph nurtured Jesus through his development and into maturity.

As he did so, Jesus "grew in wisdom and stature and in favour with God and man" (Luke 2:52). Jesus' physical, mental and intellectual development all point to him being securely attached. He was confident in engaging with the Elders at the temple. He was curious and teachable, always seeking to grow in his understanding and knowledge. He understood that he also had a deep spiritual connection to his heavenly father. Yet, he was sensitive to the needs and feelings of his earthly parents and followed their commands and leadership. Jesus demonstrates how a securely attached child can confidently explore and grow while maintaining a robust and respectful relationship with their caregivers.

Secure attachment to his heavenly father

Jesus lived a life fully embraced by God's love and guidance. His perfect example of secure attachment demonstrates practical applications for our own lives, empowering us to build a deeper, more intimate relationship with God.

These traits of secure attachment are also present in Jesus' relationship with his heavenly father. Jesus' relationship with God provides us with the ultimate example of secure attachment, characterised by trust, reliance and emotional closeness:

- <u>Deep connection to his father in prayer:</u> In several passages of Scripture (e.g. Luke 5:16), we read how Jesus withdrew to a solitary place to pray on his own. He was entirely dependent on God for strength, guidance and wisdom. And he gave us an indication of what and how he prayed during those times. We must establish a daily routine of prayer and mindfulness, just as Jesus did. In the Lord's Prayer, Jesus mentions the need for daily bread, emphasising that this is not only about physical nourishment but also spiritual sustenance from God's words (Matthew 4:4), as he made clear when responding to the devil in the wilderness. The Gospels record many times when Jesus prayed, including giving thanks, before making big decisions and when he was distressed. This was his way of staying close to God, one of the essential elements of secure attachment.

- <u>Sense of self-worth:</u> A securely attached person remains connected, optimistic and has a positive self-image. We see evidence of this in Jesus' life, particularly regarding his confidence in his identity and mission. This comes first through a declaration from his heavenly father. At Jesus' baptism, God speaks from heaven saying, "This is my Son, whom I love; with him I am well pleased." This statement is so positive and affirming and shows the closeness of their relationship. God clearly delights in him. Jesus confidently identifies himself as God's son and knows his mission.: "For even the Son of Man came not to be served but to serve others and to give his life as a ransom for many." (Mark 10:45) The fact he came to exhibit servant leadership in his ministry shows how little emphasis he places on titles and positions. He does not need recognition from men. He knows who he is. He knows who his father is. He also has confidence in the purpose and mission he came to earth to fulfil. His security, acceptance and significance come solely and uniquely from his heavenly father.

- <u>Emotional closeness and vulnerability:</u> The Garden of Gethsemane best shows Jesus' vulnerability and capacity to express his emotions. This episode in Jesus' life comes just before his arrest and crucifixion. He knows what will happen next. He sees the enormity of the task that lies before him. And he is human. He feels scared. He says to his disciples in Matthew 26:38, "My soul is overwhelmed with sorrow to the point of death." So, he turns to his father and expresses his feelings in prayer.

Jesus' prayer in the garden of Gethsemane contains a lament, a passionate expression of grief and sorrow. He prayed and asked God if any other way could be found to achieve the aim of bringing salvation to people. Understandably, he dreads enduring so much pain and suffering, even knowing it will work out in the end. Yet, he knows this is the plan God set before time began. He simply expressed to his father how difficult he found the prospect of facing this.

- <u>Trust and Obey:</u> In the second half of Jesus' prayer in Gethsemane, he exemplified trust and obedience, hallmarks of secure attachment. Jesus trusted God's plan and obeyed even unto death: "Not my will be done, but yours" (Matthew 26:39). His trust in and obedience to God's plan did not waver. Similarly, elsewhere in John's Gospel, he told his disciples, "I only do what I see the Father doing" (John 5:19). This also showed his complete alignment with God's actions and will, indicating a deep connection and an understanding that his behaviour modelled after the Father's actions. Just as children with secure attachments imitate their caregivers, Jesus modelled his actions after God the Father.

Pause for thought

In *The Bible with Nicky and Pippa Gumble*, on day 98, when commenting on a section of the Sermon on the Mount about worry, Nicky Gumble says trust and obedience are "a very good summary" of the Christian life. He says "they are the answer to trials, temptation, worry, anxiety, fear, failure and all the other struggles of life."

- Do you identify with any of these struggles with worry, anxiety, or fear of failure?

- Might these struggles relate to your attachment style and childhood relationships?

- Are you beginning to feel hopeful you can work through these insecurities using the tools we have identified?

Jesus encourages us to "seek first his kingdom and his righteousness, and all these things will be given to you as well" (Matthew 6:33). As we step out in faith and obedience, seeking Jesus' kingdom and his righteousness, Jesus tells us how we can trust that God will provide for all of our needs and not leave us wanting. If we are securely attached, like it did for Jesus this should come naturally. If we struggle with an insecure attachment style, this may not be as easy as it sounds. Still, there is a promising hope for things to be different moving forward.

- <u>Resilience:</u> Jesus endured many trials during his ministry. This began with the devil's temptations in the wilderness. On all three occasions when Satan tempted him, Jesus replied similarly: "It is written" (Matthew 4:4,7 and 10). He used the word of God, which could be paraphrased as: "Well, my Dad says…" This sits in stark contrast to the confrontation between Satan and Eve in the Garden of Eden, where Satan questions: "Did God really say?" (Genesis 3:1). Humankind struggled to take God at his word whereas Jesus stood on the word of God and quoted it at every opportunity. He faced these temptations with unwavering faith in God the Father, showing how securely attached to God he is. The same holds true of his death and resurrection, which he faced with tremendous resilience. He might have expressed pain and sorrow along the way, but "For the joy set before him, he endured the cross." (Hebrews 12:2)

- <u>Fear of being apart:</u> While hanging on the cross, Jesus quoted Psalm 22, crying out, "My God, My God, why have you forsaken me?" The sense of separation from his father was weighing upon his shoulders. He did not use the usual intimate term Abba but referred to him as God. Jesus was experiencing separation from God the Father for the first time. Before the incarnation, Jesus had had a continuous relationship with God the Father and with the Holy Spirit from the beginning of time. Now, Jesus expresses the depth of the pain of separation as this perfect, secure attachment suffered temporary disconnection. Sin separated Jesus from God so we could be brought back into right relationship with him. I don't think we can begin to imagine how that might feel. Nor can we conceive of the level of trust it takes to go through with this, confident the Father will bring him back and, in three days, restore that which has been lost.

A model for believers to follow

Jesus' relationship with God the Father exemplifies secure attachment through his trust, open communication, emotional closeness, sense of security, consistent obedience and resilience. These traits highlight the depth of their relationship and serve as a model for believers seeking a secure and intimate relationship with God. Surely, we should expect this since Jesus is the son of God. They had a special relationship. Again, this holds true. But Jesus lived like us, was made one of us and was tempted in every way just as we are. He set aside his majesty and his divinity to be made fully human. His relationship with God the Father was as a man, filled with and empowered by the Holy Spirit. In the same way he learned to form early bonds of attachment with Mary and Joseph, he also learned to form a secure attachment to God.

We can go wrong when we seek to put people on a pedestal and think they are somehow different to us. We do this to justify how we think and feel about our own inadequacies and shortcomings. We can so easily seek to put Jesus in a separate box. We believe that because he was and is God, he had unique qualities which made it easier for him to connect to God, fulfil God's purpose and mission in life and resist temptation as he did. Jesus' humanity, however, meant that he experienced life's challenges, emotions and temptations just as any other person would. The key to his extraordinary life and actions lies in his perfect, secure attachment to God the Father as a man. This attachment was characterised by deep trust, continual communication through prayer, complete submission to God's will and reliance on the Holy Spirit. His life serves as a model for believers, showing how through a secure attachment to God, we can live a life of faith, obedience and extraordinary impact. Thus, while Jesus' divine nature was essential to his role as Saviour, his humanity and secure attachment to God played a crucial role in his earthly ministry, making him a relatable example for all believers.

Lessons from Jesus' connection to his father

Accordingly, Jesus teaches us how living a life worthy of the calling upon us comes through close connection to God the Father. If he can live such an extraordinary life that flows from his connection to God, then we can aspire to it as well. At its heart lies the development of a daily routine of mindfulness and prayer. Here, we see the impact of such a routine on Jesus' life. His prayer life was how he started early each day. Jesus' special time of connection to God set him up for the rest of the day, though, in fairness, he didn't just pray first thing. He lived a life of constant prayer and connection to his dad. And in those times of worship, he bore his soul to God. He gave thanks for every good gift he received. He sometimes mourned and lamented from a place of grief and sorrow. At others, he also expressed joy and amazement. He was emotionally vulnerable and open in all of his communication with God.

Then, as his day progressed, he did what he saw the Father doing. He lived in complete trust and obedience in God's good plan for his life and the impact his life would have on others. He also ministered from a place where he received his sense of significance, acceptance and security from God. He didn't need the praise of men. He did not need any affirmation other than what God gave him. He operated from a secure base provided to him by God. The security freed him from other people's agendas, people-pleasing and other distractions from his principal mission and vision. He focused intentionally on every aspect of his life and ministry. Still, he also allowed himself to be interrupted to have compassion on someone who presented to him in need. And he overcame trials, temptations and hardships by leaning into his dad, who was also his safe haven, help in times of need and comfort as God helped him organise his feelings.

Jesus' relationship with God the Father exemplifies secure attachment through his trust, open communication, emotional closeness, sense of security, consistent obedience and resilience.

These traits not only highlight the depth of their relationship but also serve as a model for us as we seek a secure and intimate relationship with God. As we strive to be like Jesus in our own lives, we can aspire to the same deep connection with our heavenly father that he modelled so perfectly.

> **Prayer**
>
> John 15:9-10: "As the Father has loved me, so have I loved you. Now remain in my love. If you keep my commands, you will remain in my love, just as I have kept my Father's commands and remain in his love."
>
> Abba Father, we thank you for the perfect relationship between Jesus and you. Help us to deepen our attachment to you, trusting in your plan and seeking you daily in prayer. Give us the strength to follow your will with unwavering faith, sharing our joys and sorrows with you. Teach us to serve others with humility and love, finding our security in our identity in you. Fill us with your Holy Spirit, empowering us to live lives of faith, obedience and impact. May we grow in intimacy with you each day.
>
> In Jesus' name, we pray. Amen.

Conclusion

As we reach the end of this part of the journey, let's take a moment to reflect on what we have learned. We've considered how our early relationships shape our lives and how understanding this can help us heal and grow. We've also seen how being spiritually adopted by God offers a new and transformative way to overcome our deepest wounds.

My heart in writing this book was that you might find hope and healing like I have. By combining elements of psychology and theology, you should hopefully better understand why you sometimes struggle in your relationships. By embracing the idea of spiritual adoption, you can find a new sense of belonging and identity as a beloved child of God. That has been my experience, and I trust it will be yours, too. If you take away one thing, remember healing is possible.

I am on a journey of healing myself. In childhood, I developed an insecure attachment style. I wrongly perceived that love, acceptance and self-worth were linked to achievement and performance. This became a "condition of worth" leading me to be convinced my primary love language was acts of service. This, in turn, meant a disconnect existed between how I was naturally inclined to give and receive love and how I thought and felt about it. Unsurprisingly, I felt disconnected and lonely both in my earthly relationships and in my connection to my father in heaven.

My journey is leading me to discover my authentic self and identity in Christ. I am growing in my understanding that I am unconditionally loved, accepted and valued. I don't need to achieve or perform to be valuable. I am more connected to myself and to some of my innermost feelings I had suppressed for years. To my surprise, I have learned how I feel loved and connected more through physical affection and touch than in any other way. I am finally getting a sense of who I am and just how very good it is to be me.

If you had asked me a couple of years ago who the person I least expected to see change was, I would have said it was me. And yet, as you can see, I have been radically transformed and healed through connection to my heavenly father. This has filled me with faith. Now I have seen the change in me, I am far less cynical and utterly convinced anyone can change and be healed through connection to the Father. This side of eternity you will never feel as though you have somehow gotten there. This constitutes a lifelong journey of discovery and pursuing personal growth. And I am learning to seek to enjoy it.

Your past doesn't have to define you. With God's love and some practical steps, you can move away from loneliness, isolation and insecurity to feeling secure and connected to God and others. Real life through stories from the Bible and personal testimonies confirm this. Characters like Joseph and David faced many of the same struggles we do. Their stories remind you that you are not alone and that God has a plan for your healing.

We don't need to be nervous about combining psychology and spirituality. As we've seen, these ideas complement each other and provide a fuller picture of how we can heal and grow. Keep exploring and applying what you've learned. Join or get stuck into your faith community, keep praying and stay open to God's love. Remember, you are deeply loved and accepted by God.

This journey towards healing and deeper intimacy with him is a lifelong adventure. And now you have some tools in your belt and the support and encouragement you need to go further than you thought were possible. Whether through prayer, journaling, or finding a supportive community, there are many ways to draw closer to God and find healing. Remember, this journey began with a familiar feeling of wanting more – more connection, more healing, more of God. This book is just the beginning. As you continue to explore these ideas, you'll find the journey goes on, full of hope.

I have attempted to write this book like a conversation between friends. We're all on this journey together; you can take it one step at a time. Healing takes time, but with God's help, a loving community and maybe, where necessary, professional intervention, you can find the peace and connection you're looking for. Thank you for travelling with me. I hope you feel inspired and equipped to continue discovering the depths of God's love and your identity as his beloved child.

Concluding Prayer

Abba Father, thank you for guiding us through this journey of healing and discovery. We are grateful for your unconditional love and for adopting us as your children. We thank you for your relationship with us, which offers us a new model of trust and intimacy with real hope for change. Thank you that in you we find security, acceptance and significance.

May your Holy Spirit continue to lead, guide, teach and encourage us as we seek to apply these truths to our lives.

May you bring a greater measure of healing into our hearts, minds, souls and bodies as our connection to you grows deeper and we become more aware of your presence with us.

May you give us the strength and the courage to confront the gremlins of our past and trust you for your provision and plans for our future.

Please fill us with hope and faith that we may see lasting change in our relationships, first and foremost, with you and each other. Help us to reflect your love to all around us, even those who may have hurt us.

Thank you, Father, for the promise of healing and transformation. We trust in your goodness and look forward to your continued work in our lives.

In Jesus' name, we pray. Amen.

Printed in Great Britain
by Amazon